DIVERGENT SOCIAL WORLDS

DIVERGENT SOCIAL WORLDS

NEIGHBORHOOD CRIME AND
THE RACIAL-SPATIAL DIVIDE

RUTH D. PETERSON AND LAUREN J. KRIVO

A Volume in the American Sociological Association's
Rose Series in Sociology

Russell Sage Foundation • New York

Library of Congress Cataloging-in-Publication Data

Peterson, Ruth D.
  Divergent social worlds : neighborhood crime and the racial-spatial divide /
Ruth D. Peterson and Lauren J. Krivo.
      p. cm. — (American Sociological Association's Rose series in sociology)
    Includes bibliographical references and index.
    ISBN 978-0-87154-693-7 (alk. paper)
  1. Crime and race—United States. 2. Cities and towns—United States.
  3. Neighborhoods—United States. I. Krivo, Lauren Joy. II. Title.
    HV6789.P48 2010
    364.2'5—dc22

                                                                        2010005914

The paper used in this publication meets the minimum requirements of
American National Standard for Information Sciences—Permanence of Paper
for Printed Library Materials. ANSI Z39.48-1992.

Text design by Suzanne Nichols.

RUSSELL SAGE FOUNDATION
112 East 64th Street, New York, New York 10065
10 9 8 7 6 5 4 3 2 1

The Russell Sage Foundation

The Russell Sage Foundation, one of the oldest of America's general purpose foundations, was established in 1907 by Mrs. Margaret Olivia Sage for "the improvement of social and living conditions in the United States." The Foundation seeks to fulfill this mandate by fostering the development and dissemination of knowledge about the country's political, social, and economic problems. While the Foundation endeavors to assure the accuracy and objectivity of each book it publishes, the conclusions and interpretations in Russell Sage Foundation publications are those of the authors and not of the Foundation, its Trustees, or its staff. Publication by Russell Sage, therefore, does not imply Foundation endorsement.

Previous Volumes in the Series

══ Forthcoming Titles ══

Atrocities, Law, and Collective Memory
Joachim Savelsberg and Ryan King

*Counted Out: Same-Sex Relations
and Americans' Definitions of Family*
Brian Powell, Catherine Bolzendahl, Claudia Geist,
and Lala Carr Steelman

*Exceptional Children, Challenged Families: Raising
Children with Disabilities*
Dennis Hogan

Family Relationships Across the Generations
Judith A. Seltzer and Suzanne M. Bianchi

Fatherhood: Public/Private Initiatives to Engage Men
William Marsiglio and Kevin Roy

Global Order and the Historical Structures of Daral-Islam
Mohammed A. Bamyeh

*Good Jobs, Bad Jobs, No Jobs: Changing Work and
Workers in America*
Arne L. Kalleberg

The Logic of Terrorism: A Comparative Study
Jeff Goodwin

*Networked for Change: Transnational and Social
Movements in a Global Era*
Dawn Wiest and Jackie Smith

*The Production of Demographic Knowledge: States, Societies,
and Census Taking in Comparative and Historical Perspective*
Rebecca Emigh, Dylan Riley, and Patricia Ahmed

*Repressive Injustice: Political and Social Processes in the
Massive Incarceration of African Americans*
Pamela E. Oliver and James E. Yocum

*"They Say Cutback; We Say Fight Back!" Welfare Rights
Activism in An Era of Retrenchment*
Ellen Reese

The Rose Series in Sociology

THE AMERICAN Sociological Association's Rose Series in Sociology publishes books that integrate knowledge and address controversies from a sociological perspective. Books in the Rose Series are at the forefront of sociological knowledge. They are lively and often involve timely and fundamental issues on significant social concerns. The series is intended for broad dissemination throughout sociology, across social science and other professional communities, and to policy audiences. The series was established in 1967 by a bequest to ASA from Arnold and Caroline Rose to support innovations in scholarly publishing.

DIANE BARTHEL-BOUCHIER
CYNTHIA J. BOGARD
MICHAEL KIMMEL
DANIEL LEVY
TIMOTHY P. MORAN
NAOMI ROSENTHAL
MICHAEL SCHWARTZ
GILDA ZWERMAN

EDITORS

Contents

About the Authors

Ruth D. Peterson is Distinguished Professor of Social and Behavioral Sciences, professor of sociology, and director of the Criminal Justice Research Center at Ohio State University.

Lauren J. Krivo is professor of sociology and criminal justice at Rutgers University.

John Hagan is John D. MacArthur Professor of Sociology and Law at Northwestern University and senior research fellow at the American Bar Foundation in Chicago.

Foreword

America's Deadly and Duplicitous Divide

JOHN HAGAN

RUTH PETERSON and Lauren Krivo's unprecedented study of nearly ten thousand American urban neighborhoods reveals a nation racially divided, with violent and deadly consequences. The depth and detail of Peterson and Krivo's findings are particularly disturbing because while the circumstances of the racial divide in America have changed in some notable ways over time, the violent consequences nonetheless reflect a continuity that has produced a mounting toll for African and Latino Americans. The result is a nation still dangerously divided by race long after W. E. B. Du Bois (1899/1973) warned that violence was only one part of the reality of more widespread racial disparities. The deadly consequences would persist, Du Bois warned, unless we addressed the pervasiveness of the disparities.

As Du Bois anticipated, and Peterson and Krivo document, there is a stubborn and entrenched nature to the social and economic disparities in America's neighborhoods. The racial disparities are so persistent that today urban America still has virtually no equally economically situated black and white neighborhoods. In particular, there are few—if any—white neighborhoods as poor as the poorest black neighborhoods. Peterson and Krivo call this an American "racial-spatial divide" that sharply separates people by segregating the places where they predominantly reside. Poverty nearly completely overlaps with race along this racial-spatial divide, and this racial concentration of poverty and other socioeconomic disadvantages lead to a racial concentration of violence. The impinging proximity of nearby neighborhoods plagued by similar social and economic circumstances magnifies these violent consequences.

Racial segregation, poverty concentration, and the magnified consequences of proximity are thus the key elements in Peterson and Krivo's
analysis of America's racial-spatial divide. It is tempting to believe that
knowing about these elements effectively provides a path to reversing
their effects, but Peterson and Krivo's findings are not reassuring. Their
historical mentor, Du Bois, was skeptical about simple solutions, and
Peterson and Krivo's comprehensive analysis also suggests reasons to
be incredulous.

Consider the complicated history of perhaps the most central factor
they analyze in relation to the racial-spatial divide: homeownership and
investment in residential loans. Readers might initially underestimate
the centrality of residential investment in Peterson and Krivo's analysis
because *Divergent Social Worlds* offers numerous important insights
about the multiple links between an overarching racial order, social conditions, and crime. Their focus on residential investment is a linchpin in
their argument about the racial order, however, and it has particular
political resonance in view of the recent American housing collapse.

With a precision and persuasiveness made possible by their exhaustive
sampling of America's neighborhoods, Peterson and Krivo specifically
estimate that in the years leading up to 2000, a one-standard-deviation
increase in the amount of housing loan dollars resulted in a nearly 9 percent lower rate of criminal violence. They are not necessarily surprised.
The association of residential loans with crime has received little attention
in previous research, they note, even though outside investments should
shore up neighborhoods in ways that reduce violence. They base their
argument in part on related research in Chicago by Robert Sampson,
who found that higher levels of neighborhood homeownership increase
social control, social trust, and collective efficacy, which in turn diminish neighborhood violence. The 1990s was a period of falling violent crime
in America, and rising homeownership and residential investment apparently produced part of this crime reduction.

Peterson and Krivo's findings about residential loans merit especially
careful consideration because they point to a potentially important means
of counteracting the long-standing and entrenched racial divide that leads
to criminal violence. That is, while the findings in *Divergent Social Worlds*
provide grounds for pessimism, the potential of neighborhood housing
investments to reduce criminal violence also offers at least the hope of a
way in which we might effectively intervene. It is important to emphasize, however, that we would need to do so with a sensible and sustained
policy for homeownership investment backed by a collective societal
sense of responsibility and resolve that is not yet apparent in this country.

The Clinton administration ostensibly set out to increase the benefits
of homeownership among the poor and minorities in the 1990s. In 1995

this administration made changes to the 1977 Community Reinvestment Act that resulted in banks being evaluated by how much lending they did in low-income neighborhoods. Fannie Mae and Freddie Mac, which were government-initiated ventures in home lending, were further encouraged to become more involved in the securitization of mortgages. In 1997 the investment firm Bear Stearns joined Freddie Mac in launching the first $385 million securitization of these loans.

Within only a few years, however, the promise of residential investment took an ominous turn, a reversal of fortune that reminds us of how treacherous and tenacious the tactics of America's racial divide are. Peterson and Krivo's data come mainly from the later years of the Clinton administration; the following Bush administration added a perhaps aptly named Dream Downpayment Initiative in 2003 that signaled the growing deregulation of mortgage lending. The financial sector learned during the Bush years how to leverage profits from deregulated lending to "subprime" borrowers. Du Bois would have anticipated the identity of the borrowers victimized by the predatory practices that emerged from this newly relaxed lending environment.

The NAACP has charged in a class action suit that more than a dozen of America's largest banks used expensive and onerous loan products, including deceptively marketed and configured subprime loans, in systematically discriminating against African American and Latino American homeowners. The NAACP sees this as a new form of housing discrimination. In the 1960s many banks drew red lines (and thus the term "redlining") on maps around black neighborhoods where they refused to even make home loans. The NAACP charged that these same banks had now targeted many of the same black neighborhoods for subprime loans, even including black middle-class homeowners who did not need them. Mortgage lenders recognized that blacks, who were historically redlined from receiving home loans, would be ready-made customers for their newly reconfigured and deceptively marketed mortgage instruments.

The growth in subprime mortgages played perniciously on the American racial divide. Nicknames for the loans warned of the pending peril: "liar" loans, "piggyback" loans, "neg am" loans, "Ninja (No Income, No Job or Assets)" loans, and "exploding" or "suicide" loans. About one-quarter of these loans nationwide were in default or foreclosure within two years of their inception.

Because institutions resold, mixed, and traded so many subprime mortgages in the secondary securitization market, it became difficult for many homeowners or anyone else to know who actually owned their loans. A national data system, Mortgage Electronic Registration Systems (MERS), facilitated this secondary market and soon held 60 million mortgages on American homes. This system made it difficult for either homeowners or regulators to track predatory lenders. Mortgage brokers worked extensively with MERS and often steered their clients to high-priced and deceptive loans. A recent *New York Times* editorial indicates that borrowers who used brokers paid added interest payments ranging from $17,000 to $43,000 for every $100,000 they borrowed.

In a series of articles, Michael Powell of the *New York Times* reported that even black households in New York City making more than $68,000 a year were almost five times more likely than whites with similar or lower incomes to hold high-interest subprime loans. The loans victimized both middle- and working-class blacks and Latinos. People of color are three times more likely to have subprime home loans, and more than half of the home loans held by people of color are high-cost loans. Advocacy groups estimate that blacks lost as much as $100 billion in home wealth even before the subprime crisis and that Latinos lost a similar amount. This pattern constitutes a form of reverse redlining.

Foreclosures on these loans have destabilized entire communities. Peterson and Krivo found that the expansion of residential loans enabled them to act as investments that stabilized low-income neighborhoods and initially reduced crime in the years leading up to 2000. The subsequent disingenuous use of these loans, however, led to foreclosures that later destabilized the same neighborhoods. This pattern is still rippling through American low-income and minority communities, turning neighborhoods where abandoned homes had steadily accumulated into virtual, and vulnerable, ghost towns.

Peterson and Krivo's book is a stunning snapshot and analysis of America's deadly and duplicitous racial divide at the turn of the new millennium. This book tells us about both the deadly terms of this divide and the tantalizing possibilities for its change, but it also describes how durable and deadly this divide is likely to remain in the absence of major changes in the surrounding social and economic circumstances. The prospects for quickly closing the American racial-spatial divide are doubtful, and the warnings of Du Bois about the pervasiveness of this divide, a half-century after his death, still seem prescient. Peterson and Krivo's book is a timely reminder of the broadly based challenges we confront.

═ Preface ═

THIS BOOK represents the culmination of a nearly twenty-year collaboration in which we first set out to understand how segregation at the city level contributes to crime among African Americans compared to whites. During this initial collaboration, we faced, and mostly overcame, a variety of challenges inherent in studying the complex social problem of racial and ethnic inequality in crime, including: (1) melding knowledge from two different subfields within sociology (Laurie is trained in social demography and Ruth in criminology) into a hybrid explanation of race and crime that would be credible to a range of scholars; (2) learning to communicate across the barriers that come from being in different areas of the field; and (3) learning to compose together at a single computer. Laughing our way through false starts, stumbling blocks, and miscommunications, we eventually learned how to work together in a more or less seamless fashion.

With each step we took and each paper we wrote, it became more and more apparent that data were not available to explore some of the most pressing issues about how and why segregation is linked with differential patterns of crime across groups. In particular, we realized that we needed crime information for local areas and for cities that varied in their degree of segregation if we were to truly understand the segregation-crime connection. No such data existed for more than a handful of cities. Thus, we embarked on the National Neighborhood Crime Study (NNCS), with support from the Sociology and Law and Social Sciences programs of the National Science Foundation (NSF). We had several goals: (1) to compile data that would allow for an "apples-to-apples" comparison of crime in neighborhoods composed of different racial and ethnic groups; (2) to investigate neighborhood crime within its city context; and (3) to examine neighborhood crime with data that were far more broad-based and generalizable than those used in prior studies. Conducting the NNCS was not easy—it took several years to complete—but the venture was successful. We were able to assemble a unique data set with information on a variety of types of street crime for thousands of neighborhoods of different colors around the country. These data provide the underpinnings of the research that we present in this book. We use them to show the highly racialized nature of neighborhood crime in U.S. urban areas and to explicate the ways in which racially organized social and geographic structural patterns (what we call the racial-spatial divide) provide the critical underpinnings for local criminal inequality.

Along the way we received a great deal of assistance. Undertaking the project would not have been possible without the NSF funding. We are particularly grateful to the program officers, Patricia White in Sociology and Doris Marie Provine in Law and Social Sciences, for making a series of generous awards that facilitated the work. They also provided wise comments on our work at conferences and in other professional settings. We have also had the benefits of institutional support from several Ohio State University (OSU) units: the Criminal Justice Research Center (CJRC), the Initiative in Population Research, the Department of Sociology, the College of Social and Behavioral Sciences, and the Center for Urban and Regional Analysis. We are particularly grateful to CJRC, which housed the data, graduate and undergraduate research assistants, and us as principal investigators. Also, OSU provided Laurie with a sabbatical in the winter and spring quarters of 2009, which helped push the book to fruition.

The accumulation of the crime data would not have been possible without the cooperation of police officials and crime analysts across the country. Words are not adequate to convey how grateful we are to these individuals and their departments. We hope that the insights stemming from their work prove the worthiness of the endeavor. Relatedly, we are grateful to our academic colleagues throughout the country who generously shared the names of their police contacts with us and sometimes delivered the data themselves. The project would never have succeeded without their help. Unfortunately, these individuals are far too numerous to mention by name.

Throughout, we had the opportunity to work with a number of graduate research associates who gave the best of their energy and commitment to assist us in all stages of the work. Seth Feinberg helped us get started and set up the tracking system that we used throughout the data collection process. Beckett Broh and Danielle Payne became our assistants for the long haul, and Stacy Armour brought new energy when everyone was beginning to tire. We give special thanks to Beckett and Stacy for their geocoding work. Danielle was with us the longest. We very much appreciate her work with the census data and other endless details. She was particularly instrumental in making sure that data collection, archiving, and analysis moved forward and that records were organized so that we would know what was done. Danielle was also a coauthor on one of the first papers from the project because of her important contributions to the substantive development of the work. Several other graduate students also contributed. Dennis Condron, Laura McCloud, and Susan Ortiz compiled and conducted data analyses at various stages of the research. Sara Bradley worked closely with us in developing the framework of the analyses that ultimately became part of this book. Her thoughtful questioning and extreme care helped make this a better project. Although Jason Whitesel did not work directly on the NNCS, he picked up the slack on many other fronts, thus making it possible for us to devote our attention to analyses and writing.

Undergraduate students were also helpful. Jamie Selhorst and Danice Brown faithfully entered data, mapped changes in census tract boundaries (before we found GIS technology), and contributed a lot of energy and hard work to help bring the project to fruition. They were joined at times by Brandy Ethridge and Michele Whitt. Both Patrick Burke and Renee Amacher provided administrative assistance at various points. We would also like to thank the administrative associates Debbie Flower-Smith and Susan Pennington for taking care of so many of the details of making purchases, getting people paid, and otherwise helping us to stay on track with the paperwork.

Numerous individuals at OSU were also instrumental in bringing the data set to fruition by providing various types of technical assistance. Merlin Marshall facilitated our work by developing user-friendly census files. This allowed for greater ease in extracting census data and combining them with the crime data. Colin Odden and Matthew Moffitt made sure that our computers and computer networks were working smoothly, both of which were essential for keeping the work process going. Wenqin Chen, Jae Yong Kim, and Jonathan Rush provided assistance with maps and GIS programming.

A number of colleagues gave us feedback and good advice about our ideas, data, methodological strategies, substantive interpretations, and writing. We did not always take their advice, but these consultations certainly made the final product stronger. Catherine Calder helped us think more clearly about how to examine the substantive nature of spatial relationships, and she provided specific methodological advice about ways to undertake such analyses. Robert Kaufman was extremely generous with his time in helping us to address a variety of methodological and statistical challenges. More times than we could count, he was willing to answer emails, talk on the phone, and meet with us to deal with any aspect of the work, from word processing to hierarchical modeling to thorny conceptual logic. No price can be put on his ability to solve problems or his patience in doing so. William Bailey read the entire manuscript and made many, many useful suggestions. Although we do not have fond memories of the red ink that covered our manuscript, we are very grateful for his thoughtful reactions. They made us work hard to improve the manuscript, even after we thought we were mainly done. We are also grateful for the positive feedback and encouraging comments he provided between the lines of critique. Insightful comments made by the anonymous reviewers also pushed us to make this a better and more readable product.

While we were engaged in the NNCS, we began working with a group of scholars whom we now refer to as the Racial Democracy, Crime, and Justice Network (RDCJN). Over the last five years, this group has met regularly to advance understanding of the linkages between race, ethnicity, crime, and criminal justice. For us and many others, the RDCJN has become an intellectual home for cutting-edge work in the exploration of how and why ethno-racial groups have differential experiences with crime and justice. From our initial presentation of research based on the NNCS during the OSU Department of Sociology's symposium on "The Many Faces of Inequality" in 2004, to presentations on chapters related to this book during recent months, individual members and the group as a whole have listened intently to us and helped us to see innovative features in our work to which we had not been attentive. As much as any others, the members of the RDCJN have appreciated this endeavor and felt our pain and pleasure in undertaking the NNCS and writing this book. They also contributed in immeasurable ways to this effort by generally making the academic enterprise and the study of a difficult topic more meaningful and fun.

Finally, we recognize the many friends and family members who have provided support to us, individually and in tandem, and put up with general neglect when we were absorbed in our work. We are especially grateful for the tremendous outpouring of love and support that came to Laurie when she wanted to dive into the writing and press this book forward, but could not. This made us even more motivated to see the book through to completion. We hope that all of you can share in the pride of this product and appreciate what we have to say.

Several individuals bear special mention for their role in making this possible. Bob is always there with his love, advice, conversation, patience, food, and many puns. His presence certainly helps make it all seem worthwhile. Also, we cannot forget the many Friday night margaritas and great dinners Bob prepared for us that helped smooth out any of the week's troubles. Alana and Leslie have been a constant throughout this work, wondering why their crazy sociology professor mother is so excited to see police department headquarters and talk about their employees by name in every city we visit. They also provided some perspective when they asked about each paper, and then about the book, and wondered why the topic always seemed to be the same—segregation and crime. It is impossible to measure the importance of their love, support, and interest in what we do and in making this endeavor worth the effort. We hope that they will see the merits of this work and take up the charge to make the world a better place in at least some of the ways that are brought to light in this book. Bill has also been there through all of the ups and downs of this endeavor. His enthusiasm about the project and the possibilities of the data collection and research helped to keep us excited about the work, even when we were clearly in the doldrums. In addition, he added to the fun by teasing us when we would not budge from the kitchen table on some Sunday afternoons. Probably most important, however, is that he saved Ruth from being kicked out of her neighborhood for having an unkempt house and yard because he took up the slack by doing all of the yard and house work and feeding her to boot.

═ Chapter 1 ═

Introduction: One Hundred Years and Still Counting

RACE, PLACE, and crime are inextricably linked, both in actuality and in the minds of the public, in the contemporary United States. The image of the crime-ridden ghetto is prevalent in popular cultural portrayals on television, in movies, and in daily news reports (Bjornstrom et al. 2010; Russell 1998; Russell-Brown 2004). This imagery conveys the notion that African American neighborhoods are to be feared and avoided while white communities are havens of safety; Latino and other nonwhite areas are less well known but potentially risky. The fact that the vast majority of residents of African American and other minority neighborhoods are never involved in serious crime does little to dispel these images. Only a few researchers dig deeper to illuminate the complex elements at the root of continued patterns of criminal inequality by race and ethnicity. This book takes up this task and reflects our mutual interest in learning why and how race and ethnicity so fundamentally shape the experiences of urban residents, including their exposure to crime.

We came to this interest from divergent paths. One of us is white and the other African American. One of us spent her youth in the 1960s and early 1970s living on the North Side of Chicago. The other migrated from the rural South during the early 1960s and spent a portion of her teenage years on the East Side of Cleveland. Anyone familiar with Chicago and Cleveland knows that what separated us was not just that we resided in different cities, but that we lived in very different social environments because of our *racial* backgrounds. Chicago and Cleveland both have long histories of racial residential segregation, with Chicago's North Side being essentially white and much of Cleveland's near East Side essentially African American.

Our personal stories reflect the experiences of many individuals living in these different types of environment. Laurie lived in a neighborhood in which she saw almost no one but other whites on the streets, in local stores, and in the grammar school and high school to which she walked

1

just two short blocks from her home. The African Americans who crossed her path on a regular basis were the few who took the bus from the South Side to work in some of the homes in the area or to attend the local high school. Crime and fear for her safety were never obvious concerns for Laurie or her family. Indeed, when she was just twelve years old she was allowed to take the bus and the "El" to downtown with her friends. And there, in Chicago's Loop, was the primary place, outside of the TV news, where she was exposed to African Americans from the South Side: the Loop was the main middle ground between the segregated white North Side and the segregated African American South Side of the city.

Ruth's childhood was spent in the rural South toward the end of the Jim Crow era. She interacted with whites in some settings (stores, their homes), but under strict rules of racial etiquette that required deference from her. Otherwise, segregation was fairly complete: separate schools, separate churches, separate buses for transportation to school, and separate accommodations (such as restrooms and swimming pools), if African Americans were accommodated at all. Street crime was not a central concern. However, African Americans could easily get in trouble with legal authorities (and with whites in general) for minor infractions of the "race rules," and this was the basis for her parents' fear for her safety, since Ruth was an inquisitive and questioning child. Her move to Cleveland brought her to a place that seemed like a world apart from her southern rural roots. Here she rode buses with whites (and did not have to sit at the back), took classes with them, ate at the same lunch counters, and worked in proximity to whites in stores and other facilities. Still, it was impossible for her not to notice that whites and African Americans departed the bus at different stops and that eventually only African Americans remained on the bus, since they lived farther out on St. Clair Avenue. In her own neighborhood, she seldom saw white faces other than rent collectors and store clerks. It was in this area that Ruth came face to face with street crime for the first time, when a burglary occurred in one of the apartments in the building where she lived, and where one of her family members was the custodian. Although she did not become preoccupied with crime, from this incident she learned valuable lessons about urban environments as places where victimization occurs and care must be taken to keep safe.

We have had many occasions to comment on the divergent social worlds in which we grew up and how things seem to have changed since then. Many of the bricks in the walls that separated us—and others of our same colors—have been loosened or removed (see, for example, Smelser, Wilson, and Mitchell 2001). The legal barriers that kept the races apart early in our lives have been eliminated. Access to opportunities for nonwhites has expanded. Some forms of overt discrimination have declined to varying degrees. Residential segregation between African Americans and whites has, on average, decreased. The number of middle-class African American families has grown. And educational attainment has been on a steady upward trajectory for all groups, but has escalated to a particularly large degree for African Americans. One might think that by now, and with these types of change, equality of circumstances and outcomes across racial and ethnic groups would be close at hand.

However, a variety of countervailing processes belie this conclusion and demonstrate that the separate experiences of our own early lives are, in many ways, still the reality in the urban United States. For example, although average levels of segregation have declined, they remain high, especially in older industrial cities like Chicago and Cleveland (Charles 2003; Logan, Stults, and Farley 2004; Wilkes and Iceland 2004). Further, deindustrialization, which began in the 1960s, stalled the expansion of opportunities; nonwhites were particularly harmed by this long-term trend because they were disproportionately employed in the traditional manufacturing industries. As William Julius Wilson (1987, 1996, 2009) makes patently clear, deindustrialization has had especially adverse effects on African American communities, where poverty concentration and joblessness have increased. In short, the patterns and social environments that characterized the Chicago and Cleveland neighborhoods of our early years are still dramatically evident in contemporary African American and white communities. In fact, from our vantage points, many racial neighborhood inequalities may have hardened rather than softened.

Further, the inequalities seen in contemporary cities have become more complex as the colors of the U.S. urban population have diversified, largely owing to an explosion of immigration from Latin America and Asia (Bean and Stevens 2003; Iceland 2009). In addition to the African American and white populations, many places now have a mix of Latinos and other groups from around the world. Laurie's old neighborhood in Chicago is a case in point. Over half of the residents of this area are now foreign-born, and Asians alone make up one-quarter of the population (Geolytics 2003). Latinos, at somewhat more than one-tenth of the community, are also present in visible numbers. Thus, immigration is reshaping the urban environment and the local conditions that should affect crime by altering the cultural and institutional fabric of many city areas. Of course, not all urban neighborhoods are equally affected by the introduction of new groups. For example, Ruth's Cleveland neighborhood has not experienced this diversification; it has been over 95 percent African American since at least 1970 (Geolytics 2003). Moreover, the economic circumstances of newly diverse communities vary considerably: many of these neighborhoods, especially those with large numbers of

Latinos, are as disadvantaged as those of their African American counterparts (Charles 2006).

Racial Structure and Neighborhood Crime

How do these separate life circumstances of whites, African Americans, Latinos, and others yield differences in neighborhood crime? We initially thought that we could answer this question by studying Columbus, Ohio, our current hometown. Coincidentally, we live in the same neighborhood just a couple of miles from Ohio State University. Our area is almost completely white, clearly middle-class, and nearly free from serious street crime. With this in mind, we set out to determine whether the absence of crime in our community was duplicated in *nonwhite middle-class* areas of the city. At the same time, we asked whether high crime was observed in both white and nonwhite *high-poverty* communities. Our basic goals were to determine whether racial composition affects the crime rates of white and nonwhite neighborhoods when differences in economic composition are not at issue, and whether there are class differences in crime *within* white and nonwhite neighborhoods.

To address these concerns we had to locate comparable middle-class and poor white and nonwhite areas within the city, but after many hours of poring over census data, we found just one African American middle-class neighborhood in Columbus. And to our surprise, there were slim choices of poor white areas, even though our city has many poor white former Appalachian residents. Thus, the composition of communities in Columbus would have made it difficult to answer our key question and could have led to erroneous comparisons that would have confounded the effects of socioeconomic conditions on crime with the apparent effects of racial and ethnic composition. When white neighborhoods, which are mainly or totally middle-class, are compared to African American neighborhoods, which are mainly working-class or poor, race-ethnic comparisons almost completely overlap with socioeconomic comparisons. This makes it impossible to determine whether differences in socioeconomic conditions are (or are not) the sources of observed differentials in neighborhood crime. Finding racially distinct but economically comparable areas was not the only problem that would have surfaced if we had tried to use our city as a research site. Studying Columbus would have limited us to comparisons of only African American and white neighborhoods. Even with a growing Latino population, this particular midwestern city has insufficient numbers of Latinos or other groups to include such communities.

As we came to grips with the fact that our own hometown would not be a suitable site for answering fundamental questions about the connections between race, place, and crime, we also recognized that this was likely to be true for most U.S. cities. Few of them have a sufficient number of middle-class minority communities to enable a comparison with middle-class white areas (Sampson 2009; Sampson, Sharkey, and Raudenbush 2008; Sampson and Wilson 1995). Conversely, few have a sufficient number of very poor white neighborhoods to compare with the relatively large number of very poor African American and other nonwhite areas. These observations provide the foundation for the arguments that frame this book. If similarly poor and well-off white and nonwhite areas are virtually nonexistent, this social fact is not a neutral by-product of the differential efforts and tastes of individuals. Rather, this widespread pattern is a direct result of a society that is structured, through residential segregation and other mechanisms, so that neighborhoods, schools, work, and other institutions provide racial and ethnic groups with differential opportunities and access to resources. Typically, this involves privileging whites over others and leaving African Americans the furthest behind. Other racial and ethnic groups are commonly placed in hierarchical positions between these two extremes.

Those seeking to understand criminal inequality (and other outcomes) among neighborhoods of different colors must begin by recognizing the interconnections between racial structure and neighborhood crime-generating conditions. In this racialized reality, whites, African Americans, Latinos, and others are highly segregated from one another in settings where social and economic circumstances are rarely comparable. Moreover, because racial and ethnic groups have substantially different abilities to distance themselves from unfavorable urban social conditions, neighborhoods of distinct colors are further differentiated by where they are located and what is near them. Crime takes place within this racialized urban landscape. As such, what appear to be race-based differentials are more likely to be products of segregated "centers" of color that embody a preponderance of disadvantages or resources that discourage or encourage criminal activity (Du Bois 1899/1973). In other words, we contend that a critical and nearly unbridgeable racial-spatial divide in social contexts pervades the United States and sets the stage for ethno-racial inequality in crime. Moreover, in a society organized along racial lines, there is no easy corrective for criminal inequality because making conditions equal is systemically elusive.

Approaches to neighborhood crime that do not take into account the larger societal context of racial structuring might also tend toward overly simple individual-level interpretations of why crime rates are much higher in nonwhite than white neighborhoods. For example, the very high levels of crime in African American communities compared to white communities may be seen as resulting mainly from a greater proclivity for crime among African Americans and hence a greater prevalence of "criminals" in African American areas. However, the dramatic and systematic patterns in the crime data examined in this book and their relationships with structured social inequality contradict such an interpretation. Instead, these patterns suggest that inequality in crime does not result from the concentration of "bad" or "good" people in certain areas but rather is a product of people being in either a disadvantaged or privileged place. That is, crime rates are higher on average in African American than in other neighborhoods, not because members of this group are more criminally oriented, but because African American communities have the highest average levels of disadvantaged social conditions owing to the role of race in structuring opportunity and community access.

The Relevance of Crime Theories

To embed our understanding of criminal inequality in a broad societal context, we join a racialized perspective with criminological theories (see chapter 2). This is a departure from prior neighborhood crime research, which draws mainly on criminological theories alone, most commonly social disorganization. The social disorganization perspective derives from the basic observation of Clifford Shaw and Henry McKay (1969) that high rates of crime and delinquency in inner-city areas persist even when the particular immigrant and ethnic groups that make up the residential population change. This is because these areas exhibit social conditions such as poverty, residential instability, and population heterogeneity that remain despite shifts in their demographic composition. Such conditions make it difficult for residents of these areas to work together to realize their common goals (the communities are socially disorganized; see, for example, Bursik and Grasmick 1993; Sampson and Groves 1989). Drawing on this logic, researchers concerned with accounting for variation in rates of crime across areas with different racial and ethnic compositions have argued that these differentials result from distinctions in levels of poverty and other forms of disadvantage (for example, Sampson and Wilson 1995).

Research has demonstrated consistent links between structural conditions and crime within local areas (Crutchfield, Glusker, and Bridges 1999; Krivo and Peterson 1996; Pratt and Cullen 2005; Sampson 1987; Sampson, Raudenbush, and Earls 1997). Scholars have also shown that a large portion of the higher crime in African American versus white neighborhoods is due to the greater prevalence of poverty and other disadvantages in African American areas (Krivo and Peterson 1996; McNulty 2001). However, research to date has not conceptualized or analyzed societal racial and ethnic stratification as integral to the generation of neighborhood criminal inequality. Instead, societal processes that lead to differences in structural conditions have been treated as outside of criminological concerns. As noted earlier, doing so ignores the fundamental "reality" that ethno-racially distinct neighborhoods are most often *not nearly* the same and not rapidly moving toward similarity. As such, prior research fails to make clear that neighborhood inequality in crime is an inevitable outgrowth of the glaring societal gulf in community circumstances.

Here we embed social disorganization theory within a racialized perspective that explicates the central importance to U.S. society of inequality in the social and economic conditions of racial and ethnic groups and their communities. Significant consequences flow from this inequality, which would be difficult to change without altering the wider racial order that privileges whites at the expense of other groups and typically leaves African Americans on the bottom social rungs. Differences in crime rates across neighborhoods of different colors are one such important consequence, which has not yet been understood in this light.

Neighborhood Crime Patterns Across the United States

How does crime differ across neighborhoods of different colors? Specifically, what are the levels and rank orderings of violent and property crime rates among white, African American, Latino, minority (African American and Latino), and integrated areas? The answers to these questions probably seem obvious based on television, newspaper, and online media reports of crime, as well as some academic articles. Yet what may seem obvious cannot be taken for granted because direct evidence of neighborhood crime patterns is sparse. Indeed, crime data for local areas within cities are not widely available. The two of us have studied these issues for Columbus, Ohio (Krivo and Peterson 1996), and Thomas McNulty (2001) has done so for Atlanta. However, exploration of these two cities—or any other city—leaves one wondering whether the conclusions apply to other places, such as Pittsburgh, Memphis, or Phoenix, with different social and racial characters and histories.

We conducted the National Neighborhood Crime Study (NNCS) to overcome the bias of single-city research (Peterson and Krivo 2010). For the NNCS, we compiled crime and other data for 9,593 neighborhoods in 91 large cities. Including many cities throughout the United States addresses the basic problem of insufficient numbers of uncommon types of communities that is typical in the racially stratified United States. Just one city, such as Columbus, may have only one or two middle-class minority neighborhoods and just a couple of poor white areas, but collectively many cities include much larger numbers of more advantaged nonwhite and disadvantaged white communities. Together, the NNCS cities are a highly diverse set of places where just under half of all residents are non-Latino whites (47 percent) and African Americans and Latinos each make up slightly more than one-fifth (22 percent each) of the population. This diversity mirrors that found in large cities throughout the United States (U.S. Bureau of the Census 2009a). Analyzing this database of crime within diverse urban neighborhoods allows for a more comprehensive documentation of the ethno-racial patterning of crime than has ever before been available. As shown in the following chapter, the results confirm that African American neighborhoods have startlingly high rates of violent crime compared to white areas and that rates for other types of communities fall between these two. Property crime, however, is much less *un*evenly distributed than violence across the five types of racially distinct neighborhoods.

A Tale in Four Parts

We tell the empirical story of how ethno-racial differences in crime result from a societal racial order of inequality by answering four fundamental questions. First, to what extent are racial and ethnic groups residentially isolated from one another in U.S. urban areas? In the vast majority of neighborhoods in metropolitan areas in the United States, whites, African Americans, or Latinos predominate (Karafin 2009). Douglas Massey and Nancy Denton (1993) have described this residential pattern as an "American apartheid" because of the degree to which African Americans are more extremely isolated from others than any other racial or ethnic group. Beginning in chapter 3, we paint a picture of the degree of residential separation among whites, African Americans, and Latinos in the large set of cities in the NNCS. A striking portrait in which disproportionate shares of all three groups—but especially whites and African Americans—live in same-race neighborhoods provides the backdrop for the evaluation of race, place, and crime that follows.

How dramatic are gaps in the social and economic character of five ethno-racially distinct types of urban neighborhoods—white, African American, Latino, minority, and integrated? The answer to this question is the second part of our empirical tale of the broad societal origins of ethno-racial criminal inequality (also presented in chapter 3). The neighborhood residential segregation described in the first part of our story is critical in reproducing the existing privileges and disadvantages that diminish or increase the potential for crime. Drawing on the characteristics pointed to in social disorganization theory, we illuminate in detail how disadvantaged social conditions (such as poverty or an absence of professional workers) vary across the neighborhood types. We also bring attention to the ways in which residential instability, local investments, and immigration distinguish communities of different colors. The data confirm that the social context of local crime is one in which the social worlds of ethno-racial groups are highly divergent, with whites experiencing extraordinary privilege and nonwhites substantial disadvantage.

The third part of our tale addresses the extent to which differences in relative disadvantage and advantage are sources of inequality in violent and property crime across the neighborhood types. This question was raised by our own distinct residential histories in Chicago and Cleveland. Violent crime in Laurie's middle-class (but now less white) neighborhood is just one-third as high, and property crime just over 60 percent as high, as it is in Ruth's highly impoverished African American community. What reductions would there be in these crime differentials in the unlikely event that social and economic parity were achieved in these two neighborhoods? We address this question through analyses in chapter 4 of neighborhood criminal inequality for the full set of areas in our data. We begin by assessing the relationship of neighborhood factors (described in chapter 3) with violent and property crime; such an analysis has not been done previously outside of single-city studies. Only if such factors broadly affect local crime can they be responsible for criminal inequality. Next, we examine the degree to which relevant neighborhood conditions contribute to the differentials in crime across the five ethno-racial neighborhood types. An additional exploration focuses on the subset of neighborhoods that are relatively comparable in their levels of advantage to assess whether racially and ethnically distinct neighborhoods with similarly low levels of adverse conditions have rates of crime that are comparably low. The findings from these analyses highlight that neighborhood structural factors are helpful in accounting for differentials in crime across neighborhoods of different colors. Yet significant racial gaps in violent crime, though not property crime, remain even when we account for such conditions, pointing to the differentials in racial privileges found in contemporary society.

How does the spatial location of neighborhoods of distinct colors perpetuate crime gaps? The answer to this question, the fourth and final part of our tale, is presented in chapter 5. In chapter 4, we examine the effects of only the internal character of communities, thereby treating them as islands disconnected from nearby areas. However, the ways in which neighborhoods are located relative to one another may protect them from, or set the stage for, crime (Heitgerd and Bursik 1987; Mears and Bhati 2006; Morenoff, Sampson, and Raudenbush 2001; Pattillo-McCoy 1999). Further, white, African American, Latino, and other nonwhite areas are surrounded by communities with very different levels of poverty, instability, investments, and the like. At the extremes, and reflecting the U.S. racial order, African American neighborhoods often are located near highly disadvantaged communities, while white areas are surrounded by neighborhoods with many resources. We consider these external contexts by analyzing the roles of the structural conditions of areas that surround individual neighborhoods for crime. The findings make clear that such external conditions are responsible for much of the inequality in crime that is not due to ethno-racial differentials in the internal character of neighborhoods.

In telling the four-part empirical story of crime in divergent social worlds, we also offer some insights on issues that are not a core part of the set of research questions with which we began. Two such issues stand out. First, by examining a large set of neighborhoods in a broad array of cities, we move beyond the predominant focus on comparisons of African American and white neighborhoods. By studying five neighborhood types, we illuminate the subtleties in the patterns and relationships that exist in a society where diversity is extensive and growing. Latino and immigrant neighborhoods have not been totally ignored in research. However, the few existing studies have focused on a handful of border cities (El Paso, Miami, and San Diego) and have tended to compare crime in Latino and African American (or black immigrant) neighborhoods, ignoring the significant contrast with whites as the most privileged group (Cancino, Martinez, and Stowell 2009; Lee, Martinez, and Rosenfeld 2001; Martinez and Nielsen 2006; Vélez 2006).

Second, because we include neighborhoods across a large set of places, we can explore, for the first time, whether the character of the cities in which communities are located affects their levels of crime. Do neighborhoods that are similar in race-ethnic composition, level of disadvantage, extent of residential instability, and the like have more crime when they are located in cities that are larger, have weaker economies, and are more segregated? Many studies have examined crime and violence across cities (see Pratt and Cullen 2005), but these lack data for smaller areas within the overall city. Our analyses show that some city characteristics contribute to neighborhood crime. For example, when the comparable neighborhoods are located in more segregated cities or in cities with a smaller manufacturing base, they have more violence.

Once we have presented the four parts of our tale, we discuss in chapter 6 the implications of the evidence. Some of the messages that come through pertain to the value of integrating ideas from different fields (criminology, urban sociology, and of course race scholarship) for advancing understanding of an issue of important theoretical and policy concern. After reading this book, it should be very clear that dif-

ferentials in neighborhood crime are not just about collections of criminally oriented individuals or community social disorganization. Rather,
crime gaps are outgrowths of the racialized order in which groups of
all colors reside. This type of broad understanding is critical for developing policies to bring the extraordinarily high crime levels that some
communities face into closer alignment with those in more privileged
communities. Thus, our results suggest that piecemeal efforts that focus
only on crime and the criminal justice system cannot alone solve the
problems of racial and ethnic community criminal inequality. Rather,
effective and lasting solutions will come only from transforming racialized systems of opportunities and access to create far greater equality in
social conditions across groups of all colors.

We offer one final note to the reader. As we put pen to paper (or, more
aptly, fingers to keyboard), our main goal was to tell a more complete
story than heretofore available about neighborhood crime and criminal
inequality. In the end, we are satisfied that we have made an important
contribution. Indeed, we believe that we might even get an approving
nod from W. E. B. Du Bois (1899/1973), who over one hundred years
ago wrote about the difficulty of explicating the complex social conditions that gave rise to the relatively high crime rate in Philadelphia's
nineteenth-century black neighborhoods. Du Bois clearly understood
how deep the racial-spatial divide runs in U.S. society, and he would
probably be chagrined that the weakening of this divide is yet to be realized. Still, we believe that he would applaud the exposure of the systemic injustices we document in this book.

Chapter 2

Racial Structure, Segregation, and Crime

VIOLENT CRIME in a predominantly African American neighborhood on the East Side of Columbus, Ohio, was a whopping 22.9 per 1,000 residents in 2000, a rate that was over twice the citywide average of 9.8. During that year, residents of this moderately poor neighborhood with nearly 4,000 residents fell victim to seventy-eight reported violent incidents, including two murders and twelve rapes.[1] Just six miles away in a moderately poor white community, the picture was somewhat rosier. There the violent crime rate was less than half the rate in the African American neighborhood at just 10.6 offenses per 1,000 population. The forty-eight total reports of violent victimization included no killings and just six rapes. In faraway Los Angeles, the pattern was much the same. A white neighborhood in the northern part of the city registered the typical rate of violence for white areas of just over five reported incidents per 1,000 residents.[2] Across town, a Latino community of similar economic status approached twice this level of violent crime: almost ten incidents per 1,000 residents were reported to the police in 2000. In this same sprawling city, an African American neighborhood with somewhat more poverty than the Latino community had a level of violence that far exceeded that in Los Angeles areas of other colors: more than thirty acts of criminal violence were reported to the police per 1,000 people.

Both casual and scientific observers of cities are convinced that these types of statistics reflect the reality of urban life in the United States for whites, African Americans, Latinos, and other groups. Most would say that, at one extreme, whites tend to live in neighborhoods where crime, particularly violent crime, is relatively uncommon. At the other extreme is the clear impression that African Americans reside in communities where reports of serious violent crime are all too frequent and property offenses are comparatively common. If considered at all, Latino neighborhoods and more mixed areas are thought to have less crime than African American localities, but to be far more plagued by this problem than areas where whites predominate.

12

Is this actually the case? Are African American neighborhoods more crime-ridden than all other types of communities? Are white communities by far the safest? Do levels of crime in Latino areas and racially mixed areas fall between those for white and African American communities? To date, we do not have solid answers to these questions other than for individual cities such as Columbus, Atlanta, and Miami (see, for example, Krivo and Peterson 1996; Kubrin and Wadsworth 2003; McNulty 2001; Morenoff, Sampson, and Raudenbush 2001; Nielsen, Lee, and Martinez 2005; Shihadeh and Shrum 2004; Wooldredge and Thistlethwaite 2003). These studies highlight for the settings they examine how communities are privileged (whites) or harmed (African Americans and Latinos) by the extensiveness of crime. However, we do not know whether these patterns are unique to the cities studied or whether they extend to urban areas throughout the United States.

In this study, we take up the challenge of exploring how patterns of neighborhood crime vary across communities of different colors for a representative set of cities across the nation. Do patterns of violent and property crime comport with what casual and scientific observers of cities believe they know about the differential distribution of urban crime for the country as a whole? The national portrait provided to answer this question shows stark neighborhood inequalities that are broadly consistent with casual impressions, particularly for violent crime. In the remaining chapters, we attempt to account for these dramatic ethnoracial differentials. We contend that the crime patterns observed are so stark that they demand recognition of the interconnections between racial structure and local crime-generating conditions. We draw on structural race theories and research, as well as arguments and evidence from structural approaches in criminology and urban sociology, to articulate such a racialized perspective.

Patterns of Race and Crime

Frequently cited statistics from a variety of sources show that there is a close connection between race and crime across *individuals* in the United States. For example, in 2007 African Americans represented 39 percent of persons arrested for violent crime and 30 percent of those arrested for property offenses, but they made up only 13 percent of the U.S. population (U.S. Department of Justice 2008a). The rate of homicide offending and victimization was six to seven and a half times higher for African Americans than for whites each year from 2000 to 2005 (Pastore and Maguire 2009a). Murder is the leading cause of death for African American males between the ages of fifteen and thirty-four, and the second leading cause of death for Latino males of these ages (National

Center for Health Statistics 2009).[3] African Americans and Latinos are more likely than whites to be victims of a range of violent and property crimes; rates of violent victimization are 23.9 per 1,000 for whites, but 28.4 and 32.9 per 1,000 for Latinos and African Americans, respectively (Pastore and Maguire 2009b). Property victimization is particularly likely among households headed by Latinos, for whom the rate is 211.7 per 1,000 compared with rates of 185.6 for African Americans and 156.7 for whites (Pastore and Maguire 2009c).

These types of statistics indicate that nonwhite *individuals* are over-represented among the ranks of crime victims and offenders. However, they do not tell us whether or how ethno-racial differentials affect communities of distinct colors. One source of evidence on the disproportionality in crime across places with varying racial and ethnic compositions is research on total, violent, and property crime for large aggregate units, including cities, metropolitan areas, counties, states, and nations. Travis Pratt and Francis Cullen (2005) have assessed the scores of journal articles (more than two hundred) published between 1960 and 1999 on aggregate crime. Many of these provided data on how racial concentration is linked to rates of offending or victimization. Pratt and Cullen find considerable evidence that crime is disproportionately concentrated in cities and other large ecological units where relatively more African Americans reside. Notably, the percentage of black (or nonwhite) residents is among the four strongest and most stable macro-level predictors of crime.

Studies that have directly examined ethno-racial inequality in crime across neighborhoods within cities show patterns that are consistent with those described at the start of this chapter for Columbus and Los Angeles. Rates of crime are higher in local areas where African Americans are more heavily concentrated and, conversely, lower where African Americans constitute a smaller portion of residents, whether in Atlanta, Baton Rouge, Chicago, Cleveland, Columbus, New York, Philadelphia, or Seattle (Crutchfield, Matsueda, and Drakulich 2006; Hipp 2007; Krivo and Peterson 1996; Logan and Stults 1999; Massey, Condran, and Denton 1987; McNulty 2001; McNulty and Holloway 2000; Messner and Tardiff 1986; Morenoff, Sampson, and Raudenbush 2001; Shihadeh and Shrum 2004). Often the differentials within individual cities are quite stark. For example, Douglas Massey, Gretchen Condran, and Nancy Denton's (1987) early study of Philadelphia showed that murder, rape, robbery, and aggravated assault rates were an average of 2.1 to 2.7 times higher in black than in white neighborhoods. Violence was particularly extreme in the seventy-five "established" black areas—neighborhoods that had remained predominantly black from 1970 to 1980. Differences in property crime by neighborhood color existed but were much less pronounced; burglary, larceny, and motor vehicle theft were 23, 16, and 31 percent higher, respectively, in all black than all white areas in Philadelphia.

More recent research shows similar patterns. McNulty's (2001) study of block groups in Atlanta in 1990 found that rates of murder were a startling six times higher in predominantly black neighborhoods than in predominantly white neighborhoods, and nearly four times as high in racially mixed areas as in white areas. Rape and robbery rates in African American areas were over three times those in white neighborhoods, and aggravated assaults were about twice as common in the former than the latter. The racially mixed neighborhoods in Atlanta had more than two times the levels of rape, robbery, and aggravated assault as white areas. Similarly, neighborhood maps of Seattle for 2002 through 2003 demonstrated that the areas with the greatest concentrations of violence corresponded with disproportionate concentrations of nonwhites (Crutchfield, Matsueda, and Drakulich 2006).

Only one study has examined levels of violence across neighborhoods of distinct colors for more than a few cities. John Hipp (2007) reports rates of aggravated assault and robbery for areas of distinct race-ethnic composition for nineteen cities spread throughout the country. These data show the familiar pattern found for individual cities: notably lower rates in white neighborhoods than in areas with any other ethno-racial composition. Such disproportionality means that the average white household lives in a neighborhood with substantially less crime than is the case for the typical African American household. This is also clearly illustrated in John Logan and Brian Stults's (1999) analysis of metropolitan Cleveland for 1990. Property crime rates were over one and a half times higher in the neighborhoods of black households than in those of white households, and rates of violent crime differed by a magnitude of nearly five.

A few studies have compared crime in Latino neighborhoods with rates for other areas. María Vélez (2006) shows that, in Chicago in 1990, homicide rates in Latino neighborhoods, at 0.43 per 1,000, were about one-half those for African American areas (0.84 per 1,000). In El Paso, Miami, and San Diego, Latino neighborhood homicide rates were 40 to nearly 70 percent lower than in African American communities (Lee, Martinez, and Rosenfeld 2001). Also, aggravated assault and robbery in Miami were most pronounced in African American neighborhoods; rates were somewhat lower in Haitian communities and lowest in Latino neighborhoods. White areas were not studied (Martinez and Nielsen 2006).

Racialized patterns of crime have also been highlighted in in-depth qualitative analyses (see Anderson 1990, 1999; Bourgois 1995; Carr 2005; Miller 2008; Pattillo-McCoy 1999; Sullivan 1989; Wilkinson 2003). For example, Elijah Anderson (1990) details life in two urban neighborhoods in Philadelphia, one poor and African American (Northton) and one racially mixed and middle- to upper-middle-income (the Village). A central aim of this study is to understand how residents of the two neighborhoods manage public space and coexist in the same general area. One core component of this public negotiation involves dealing with criminal assaults and the drug trade on the streets of Northton and the Village. The centrality of drugs and violence to Philadelphia's African American neighborhoods is shown even more poignantly in *Code of the Street* (Anderson 1999). In this book, Anderson documents the lives of young men in depressed and racially isolated neighborhoods who are unable to rely on the police and who therefore develop codes for street life that call for the use of violence to protect themselves, their self-respect, and others. Deanna Wilkinson (2003) examined violent events among African American and Latino male youth and young adults in two very poor neighborhoods in New York City. Like Anderson, she demonstrates that widespread interpersonal violence emerges as a means for young people to manage everyday life in communities where disenfranchised minority youth feel that they cannot rely on the police for protection. In particular, carrying weapons and taking on a tough demeanor, which set the stage for violent encounters, are seen as necessary to achieving respect in a context where legitimate opportunities for status are severely lacking.

Jody Miller's (2008) dramatic portrait of the life of girls in a neighborhood in North St. Louis shows that the pervasive violence in extremely impoverished African American areas is not limited to males. In a context where resources and high social status are limited, street respect takes on critical importance. Violence against young women, particularly sexual violence at the hands of males, becomes intricately interconnected with attempts to define masculinity and gain respect. As Miller notes (2008, 192), "Urban African American young women face widespread gendered violence that is a systematic and overlapping feature of their neighborhoods, communities, and schools." Nikki Jones (2009) also discovered that participation in violence by African American girls in inner-city Philadelphia is necessary for self-protection and to gain respect.

Other qualitative neighborhood studies show that concerns about violent and property crime go beyond heavily disadvantaged African American areas. Mary Pattillo-McCoy (1999) draws attention to the heightened risk of crime and violence in a middle-class black community in Chicago stemming from its location near other African American areas that are more troubled. Race-based patterns of segregation that limit the neighborhood residential options of even middle-class African Americans produced this situation. In contrast, Patrick Carr (2005) demonstrates that residents of a white working-class neighborhood in Chicago are able to fend off potential encroachments of crime, violence, and gangs from nearby areas by participating in organizations that form alliances with institutions, such as the city council and the police, that can intercede in conflicts and provide problem-solving resources such as zoning rules and recreation programs that serve as mechanisms of social control. Carr suggests that nonwhite and impoverished neighborhoods may lack experience with and access to such public-sphere goods and services.

How representative are the patterns of crime reported in past research? The consistency of the results suggests that what is assumed to be broadly true about criminal inequality across neighborhoods of distinct colors is correct. Yet the evidence is piecemeal and may not be representative of the diverse types of cities and neighborhoods found throughout the United States. To undertake a more systematic assessment we conducted the National Neighborhood Crime Study, in which we collected data for a sample of large U.S. cities. The NNCS includes crime data reported to police departments for neighborhoods in 91 cities with populations of 100,000 or more persons for the year 2000. Drawing on these data, we present portraits of violent and property crime across neighborhoods of distinct colors for nearly 9,000 local areas throughout the United States to provide the broad documentation that has been lacking to date. We make comparisons across five types of ethno-racial neighborhoods: predominantly white, predominantly African American, predominantly Latino, minority, and integrated. (See chapter 3 for formal definitions of the neighborhood types.)

Figures 2.1 and 2.2 present these comparisons for rates of violent crime (murders and robberies) and property crime (burglaries, larcenies, and thefts of motor vehicles), respectively. Rates are defined as the total number of violent or property crimes in a neighborhood per 1,000 persons residing in the area. The figures present mean rates for each ethno-racial neighborhood type, as well as the values that include the middle 50 percent of all rates (twenty-fifth percentile and seventy-fifth percentile). The end points of each line show the fuller range of rates for each neighborhood type by indicating the values below and above which only 10 percent of all cases fall (tenth percentile and ninetieth percentile). First and most striking, inequality in *violent crime* across different-color neighborhoods is dramatic (figure 2.1). The average rate of criminal violence for African American neighborhoods of 10 per 1,000 population is five times that for white areas, where the mean is just 2 per 1,000 residents. The average violence rate for minority areas (7.1 per 1,000) is over three and a half times that for white neighborhoods. And typical Latino (4.9 per 1,000) and integrated (4.8 per 1,000) communities have nearly two and a half times as much violent crime as their white counterparts. Thus, differentials in mean rates for neighborhoods in a broad and representative set of places are at least as great as those found for black and white areas in Philadelphia

Figure 2.1   Violent Crime Rates for Neighborhoods of Different Colors

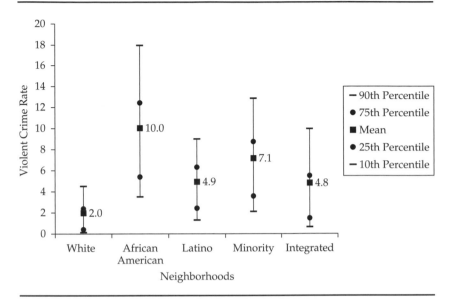

Source: National Neighborhood Crime Study (Peterson and Krivo 2010).

Figure 2.2   Property Crime Rates for Neighborhoods of Different Colors

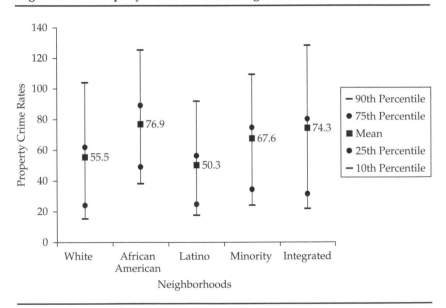

Source: National Neighborhood Crime Study (Peterson and Krivo 2010).

(Massey, Condran, and Denton 1987) and Atlanta (McNulty 2001) for earlier periods. We also observe large gaps in average violence rates between Latino and African American neighborhoods, as do Vélez (2006) and Ramiro Martinez and his colleagues (Lee, Martinez, and Rosenfeld 2001; Martinez and Nielsen 2006) for just a few cities (Chicago, El Paso, Miami, and San Diego).

Figure 2.1 also shows the degree of overlap in levels of violent crime across the five neighborhood types. The contrast between African American and white areas is particularly striking. Only about 20 percent of African American neighborhoods have levels of violence that are as low as the rates found in 90 percent of white communities (ninetieth percentile). Rates of violence are so great in many African American areas that a full one-quarter experience levels that also exceed those in most other nonwhite or integrated communities. There is considerable overlap in violence levels among Latino, minority, and integrated neighborhoods (although rates rise higher in minority neighborhoods than in the other two types of communities). There is also greater correspondence in the levels of violence for these three types of areas with white localities than for African American neighborhoods. However, this overlap belies the point that more than one-quarter of white areas have rates of violence that are lower than those found in 90 percent of Latino, minority, and integrated communities.

Turning to property crime in figure 2.2, note first that rates are considerably higher for property crime than for violent crime, as is consistently the case in the United States (U.S. Department of Justice 2008b). Moreover, inequality in property crime across ethno-racial neighborhoods is much less pronounced than for violent offenses. Average property crime rates vary from a low of 50 per 1,000 population in Latino areas to a high of 77 per 1,000 residents in African American neighborhoods (a difference of slightly more than 50 percent). Consistent with the similarity in means, there is also substantial overlap in neighborhood rates of property offenses. Indeed, the Latino and minority distributions overlap almost completely with whites' and with each other. Nonetheless, about half of white neighborhoods (median = 39.2) have property crime rates below those in virtually all (90 percent) African American areas. The only other pattern of note is that rates for integrated neighborhoods tend to reach the higher levels observed for African American areas.

The dramatic inequality found in these national data, particularly for violent crime, highlights the need for a racialized perspective to understand ethno-racial differentials in neighborhood crime. Indeed, our statistical evidence calls for a framework that articulates the social context of racial stratification that generates such inequality. Certainly, neighborhood ethno-racial composition itself is not the *cause* of the observed criminal differentials. Appropriate interpretation of the sources of these gaps must come from a social theory that specifies the structural conditions that produce them (Bonilla-Silva and Zuberi 2008; Zuberi 2001; Zuberi and Bonilla-Silva 2008a, 2008b). In the following sections, we present such a theoretical framework. Our perspective emphasizes how a racialized society produces highly inequitable environments that create and re-create divergent levels of crime across neighborhoods that are distinct in their racial and ethnic makeup.

The Racial Structure of Society

Many social science and legal scholars contend that race is a key organizing principle within and across societies (Bobo 2004; Bonilla-Silva 2001, 2003; Feagin 2000; Marable 2004; Omi and Winant 1994). This view has taken on increasing prominence in recent decades as scholars have theorized and studied "the qualitative differences between white and non-white groups' encounters with U.S. society [or] to put it another way . . . the extent to which U.S. society is racially structured from top to bottom" (Omi and Winant 1994, 49–50). Among critical race legal theorists, "realists" contend that racism is not merely a set of unfavorable thoughts, words, and attitudes toward some groups, but rather the means by which society allocates privilege and status in a racially hierarchical manner (Delgado and Stefancic 2001). Such an orientation has also been applied by social scientists writing about various topics, including politics, education, religion, and methods of research (see, for example, Bobo 2004; Bonilla-Silva 2001, 2003; Dawson 1994; Edwards 2008; Forman and Lewis 2006; Lewis 2003; Marable 2003; Matsueda and Drakulich 2009; Zuberi 2001; Zuberi and Bonilla-Silva 2008b).

What does it mean to argue that society is racially structured? Eduardo Bonilla-Silva (2001, 2003) provides a widely cited answer to this question. He contends that U.S. society and many other societies are racialized social systems in which political, social, economic, and ideological aspects of society are partially structured along racial lines. This organization is hierarchical, with one racial group (or groups) being dominant and the clear beneficiary of societal rewards. Other groups are subordinate and concomitantly disadvantaged. Specifically,

> the race placed in the superior position tends to receive greater economic remuneration and access to better occupations and prospects in the labor market, occupies a primary position in the political system, is granted higher social estimation (e.g., is viewed as "smarter" or "better looking"), often has the license to draw physical (segregation) as well as social (racial etiquette) boundaries between itself and other races, and receives what W. E. B. Du Bois called a "psychological wage." (Bonilla-Silva 2001, 37)

This type of social system is maintained through the racial distinctions made in everyday interactions and institutional practices. These actions vary over time and across place and may be more or less overt (for example, Jim Crow laws, housing discrimination, inequitable school funding, and differential law enforcement). However, racial inequality in opportunities and rewards is a constant in a racialized social system. Such race-based differences are self-perpetuating because groups that receive varying rewards have distinct group interests. The privileged racial group has much to gain from keeping its superior position and just as much to lose from the elimination of racial inequality. Therefore, those in a dominant position act to maintain their benefits by preserving rather than challenging the status quo. Subordinate groups seek to change their position in the system but often lack the power to do so.

Bonilla-Silva's core contention is that the foundation of racial inequality is structural rather than individual in nature. Differential outcomes across ethno-racial groups are not produced by individual actions based on prejudice or racial animus. Rather, they result from social relations and practices that are racially patterned, whether intentionally or not. Bonilla-Silva is not the only scholar who emphasizes the structural underpinnings of racial inequality. Michael Omi and Howard Winant (1994, 60) underscore that, in the United States, individuals are "inserted in a comprehensively racialized social structure." At the macro level, this has substantial implications for interpreting the meaning of race in society and for framing political "projects" that seek to uphold or attack the racial order.[4] Joe Feagin (2000) describes the United States as a "total racist society" with deep historical roots that are systemic in nature. For him, this means that racism is structured into every part of society, including the economy, criminal justice, politics, education, religion, and the family. This core racist reality is reproduced by institutional and individual discrimination and through relationships of oppression that create distinct interests for whites (the dominant group) and blacks (the oppressed racial group on which Feagin first focuses). Manning Marable (2003) holds a similar view when he describes the American state as having been founded on a racial foundation that continues to underpin the social and political structure of the United States. Thus, he notes, persistent racial inequalities in social outcomes are the product of structural barriers against nonwhites alongside pervasive white privilege in access to power and resources.[5]

The racialized social structure is clearly seen in the organization of opportunities and resources that maintain white privilege and minority oppression in a wide range of institutions. Schools, the labor market, politics, criminal justice, health care, and the like are structured in ways that reinforce a hierarchy of access and rewards across populations of color, with whites garnering the highest-quality institutional resources. This includes disproportionate opportunities to attend the best schools, obtain prestigious jobs, gain political and legal representation, and gain access to high-quality medical care. As a result, whites typically accrue the greatest rewards from institutional resources—for example, higher income, better education, superior health, more efficient police service, and greater wealth. To illustrate, public schools are generally funded at the local level by property taxes. This produces large differentials in school resources across communities with varying economic and racial compositions (Grant-Thomas and powell 2009; powell 2007). The typical school in a predominantly white community has better physical facilities, more experienced teachers, more advanced course offerings (such as Advanced Placement high school classes), and lower student-teacher ratios than is the case in urban minority areas (see McKoy and Vincent 2008; Reskin 2004; Roscigno 1998; Solorzano and Ornelas 2002). The individual and community consequences of such inequalities are striking. Vincent Roscigno (1998) shows that many of these factors are associated with higher achievement in mathematics and reading. School segregation is additionally connected with achievement: students in high schools that are nearly completely white have significantly higher school performance, and those in schools with predominantly black student bodies have lower test scores, than individuals in more racially mixed schools.

Ethno-racial inequality in education feeds into the labor market, where it contributes to differentials in levels of employment, occupational status, and earnings (Conrad 2001; Holzer 2001; Kaufman 2001). However, the labor market itself provides inequitable opportunities and outcomes that go beyond the inputs that emanate from school systems (and other institutions). For example, racial segregation in the labor market is pronounced (see, for example, Jacobs 2001; Kaufman 2001; King 1992; Tomaskovic-Devey 1993). Robert Kaufman (2001, 2010) shows that about one-fifth of whites (or blacks) would have to change their jobs for these two racial groups to have the same distributions across labor market positions. This level of job segregation holds *after* accounting for differences between racial (and gender) groups in characteristics such as education, marital status, urban residence, and regional location (see also Anderson and Shapiro 1996; Dodoo and Kasari 1995). Such segregation has a large influence on inequality in earnings. Racial labor market segregation accounts for about one-third of the lower earnings of black men compared to white men and produces more than a $2,000 difference in the earnings of black versus white women (Kaufman 2001).

Racial stratification is also evident in the operations of criminal justice institutions (see, for example, Chan and Mirchandani 2002; Jiwani 2002; Marable, Steinberg, and Middlemass 2007; Mauer 2009). Though the form and degree vary, racialized patterns of justice occur at every stage of processing, including lawmaking, policing, prosecutorial and judicial proceedings, and imposition and release from punishment. The criminal justice laws and procedures that have served as tools for the preservation of whites' advantage over other race and ethnic groups from the colonial period forward include: legal slavery; the criminalization of behaviors that are common among subordinate groups but not among whites, such as running away during slavery, Jim Crow laws, and crack versus powder cocaine laws; differential policing in racial profiling, arrest decisions, and the use of deadly force; the imposition of harsher penalties for crimes if committed by racial minorities, especially if they involve white victims (see, for example, Spohn 2009; Walker, Spohn, and DeLone 2007); and the use of lynching as punishment for presumed violations or to deter those who might threaten whites' interests, often with the tacit approval of criminal justice agencies (Delgado 2009; Gonzales-Day 2006; Pfeifer 2004; Tolnay and Beck 1995).

Drug laws and policies exemplify the criminal justice mechanisms that serve to control "other" populations and preserve white privilege during times of perceived threat from encroachments by subordinate groups. Several early drug laws are illustrative. The Harrison Narcotics Act of 1914, the Marihuana Tax Act of 1937, and the Comprehensive Drug Abuse Prevention and Control Act of 1970 were responses to perceived threats to dominant groups from nonwhite populations during periods of economic downturn or shifts in power relationships between whites and nonwhites. Drug use by Chinese workers, blacks in the South, and Mexican workers in the West symbolized the problems associated with labor surpluses during difficult economic times, shifting cultural patterns, and, in the case of the 1970 act, the possibility that existing drug laws would imprison the "cream of white youth" (see Musto 1973; Peterson 1985; Provine 2007; Reasons and Perdue 1981). Consistent with earlier periods, recent drug law policies have been described as a "race-conscious war on urban black and, to a lesser extent, Latino communities" (Marable 2007, 5; see also Provine 2007). One of the main features of the Reagan administration's "War on Drugs," launched in 1986, was substantially longer prison terms for the possession and sale of crack cocaine—a drug commonly used by black inner-city residents, though they were a small portion of the illicit drug–using population—than for these same actions with powdered cocaine, which, along with marijuana, was the illicit drug of choice of white users, who were also the overwhelming majority of drug users. Another feature of the drug war was aggressive policing, such as "buy and bust" strategies, massive street sweeps, the establishment of "drug-free zones," and the like. These types of policies have all had a disparate impact on minorities and their communities (Beckett, Nyrop, and Pfingst 2006; Greene, Pranis, and Ziedenberg 2006; Marable 2007).

A variety of contemporary policing and prosecutorial policies, such as "three strikes" laws, "truth in sentencing" legislation, and juvenile transfer to adult courts, also have a disproportionate impact on African Americans and Latinos (Bortner, Zatz, and Hawkins 2000; Chen 2008; Ehlers, Schiraldi, and Lotke 2004; Fagan and Zimring 2000). Further, Latinos are racialized in criminal justice by being associated with immigrant communities that, in some places, have been constructed as sites of crime and other social problems (Romero 2006; Zatz and Smith 2008). As such, whether they are citizens or not, Latinos may be more likely to be arrested, prosecuted, and subjected to other criminal procedures to deal with perceived problems associated with immigration.

Racially differentiated opportunities, punishments, and rewards in education, the labor market, and criminal justice do not operate completely independently of one another or of other institutions in creating and perpetuating the racial order (see, for example, Grant-Thomas and powell 2009; Reskin 2004). Rather, advantages or disadvantages in one or more institutions can be mutually reinforcing as they further privileges for whites and detrimental outcomes for African Americans, Latinos, and others. As already noted, whites have disproportionate access to communities with the best public schools. Higher-quality educational programs in elementary through secondary schools improve the likelihood of high school completion, which, in turn, substantially reduces the chance of ending up in prison (Western 2006). Superior community educational resources also improve access to college, thereby increasing prospects for obtaining jobs with higher prestige, earnings, and benefits. Residence in local areas with "good schools" has effects beyond direct and indirect educational benefits; because home values are greater in such communities, residents accrue more wealth through equity in their residence (Oliver and Shapiro 2006; Shapiro 2004). Wealth can help to finance college and other investments that garner continued returns through retirement and across generations (Conley 1999; Shapiro 2004).

In contrast, African Americans, Latinos, and other nonwhites experience significantly lower life chances throughout a host of institutions. These disadvantages accumulate and help solidify the position of these groups at (or near) the bottom of the social hierarchy. For instance, segregation increases the likelihood that African Americans will live in local areas with low-quality school districts (McKoy and Vincent 2008). The resulting concentration of African Americans in communities with struggling schools creates the opposite spiral of that observed for whites. Constrained school access increases high school dropout rates and reduces levels of college attendance, both of which lead to higher rates of incarceration (Western 2006). Young people emerging from such environments are more likely to end up in low-prestige jobs with associated low incomes. The quality of local schools and the concentration of African Americans (or Latinos) are also associated with lower home values and less potential to accumulate housing wealth, with its attendant benefits (see, for example, Flippen 2004).

The racialized policies and practices of the criminal justice system also reverberate through other institutions in ways that create enormous harm for nonwhite individuals and communities. To date, they have contributed to widespread growth in the prison population, which has disproportionate numbers of African Americans and Latinos (Clear 2007; Marable 2007; Western 2006). Notably, approximately two-thirds of persons incarcerated for a drug offense in America's state prisons and three-quarters of those incarcerated on federal drug charges are either African American or Latino; these figures far exceed the proportion of these groups among the U.S. population, as well as among drug users and sellers (Marable 2007; Mauer 2009; Western 2006). Following from imprisonment are poor job prospects (especially if one is African American), relatively low earnings, voting disenfranchisement (in many states), and diminished civic participation (Manza and Uggen 2006; Pager 2007; Western 2006). Difficulties in the labor market, in turn, affect a host of additional life chances, including family formation, marital stability, residential location, homeownership with attendant implications for wealth accumulation and school quality, and voting and other forms of civic participation (Western 2006). High rates of imprisonment also have devastating consequences for communities that experience vicious cycles of residents churning in and out (Clear 2007). When incarceration and the churning of offenders reach very high levels, these processes heighten social disorganization and reduce social capital, which, in turn, increase crime. Because African Americans and Latinos are vulnerable to racialized criminal justice policies, disadvantaged communities populated by these groups feel these effects most acutely. To the extent that social disorganization is heightened, the disparate policies of the criminal justice system make it at least partially responsible for the very crimes that it purports to reduce.

The argument that racially inequitable patterns are embedded within and across institutions does not preclude the possibility of variation in achievement *within* racial groups. Nor does it call into question evidence of upward mobility and growth in the middle class among African Americans, Latinos, and other groups (Bean et al. 2001; Oliver and Shapiro 2006; Pattillo-McCoy 1999; Shapiro 2004; Smith and Horton 1997; U.S. Commission on Civil Rights 2005). Indeed, after the civil rights movement and related legislation, the proportion of black households with middle-class incomes increased through the early 1980s (Oliver and Shapiro 2006; U.S. Commission on Civil Rights 2005). In addition, the percentage of black individuals employed in professional and managerial occupations grew from 4.7 percent in 1960 to 8.4 percent in 2007 (U.S. Bureau of the Census 1962, 2009b).[6] Frank D. Bean and his colleagues (2001) show appreciable gains from 1979 through 1998 among *native-born* Latino households with middle-class incomes. This group also saw a 44 percent increase in the level of college completion (from 10.7 percent to 15.4 percent) over the same period.

These gains for African Americans and Latinos notwithstanding, middle-class status does not have the same meaning for whites and for racial-ethnic minorities in the United States. For example, the circumstances of families and individuals in the black and Latino middle classes are considerably more precarious than those for the white middle class. African Americans are concentrated in lower-middle-class occupations and have less wealth and fewer other economic resources to fall back on than whites do (Oliver and Shapiro 2006; Pattillo-McCoy 1999; Shapiro 2004; Smith and Horton 1997; U.S. Commission on Civil Rights 2005; see also Lacy 2007). College-educated native Latino males also received much lower income returns to their education than native white males, and they contributed to the support of larger households (Bean et al. 2001; Bean and Stevens 2003). Thus, social position, even for middle-class African Americans and Latinos, reflects the systemic ways in which race permeates U.S. society.

Residential Segregation: A Structural Mechanism

The goal of this book is to show the critical role of the hierarchical racial system described here in generating ethno-racial inequality in neighborhood crime patterns. In the United States, residential segregation and the organization of the housing market that supports continued segregation are key mechanisms that undergird the existing hierarchy and lead to neighborhood differences in outcomes, including crime (Bonilla-Silva 2001; Massey and Denton 1993). Here we articulate the sources and levels of ethnic and racial residential segregation in the United States and explain how it is linked with structurally inequitable neighborhood environments for whites, African Americans, Latinos, and others. Our key contention is that residential segregation is the linchpin that connects the overall racial order with dramatic racial and ethnic differentials in violent and property crime across communities. It does this by reinforcing the complicated web of social and institutional inequalities that privilege white neighborhoods compared to African American, Latino, and other types of neighborhoods. Segregation is thus at the heart of why the social worlds of people in the United States are so divergent by neighborhood color, and hence why neighborhood crime is so racialized.

What forces underlie residential segregation in urban areas of the United States? The long U.S. history of housing market discrimination by race and place created and has reinforced race-ethnic segregation (Charles 2003; Gotham 2002a, 2002b; Massey and Denton 1993; Pager and Shepherd 2008; Ross and Turner 2005; Yinger 1995). Historical policies and practices, including restrictive covenants and Federal Housing Administration/Veterans Administration (FHA/VA) lending policies (such as redlining and minimum unit and lot standards), supported the development of white neighborhoods and suburban localities (see, for example, Jackson 1985; Massey and Denton 1993). FHA and VA loans provided major financing for the expansion of homeownership that took place before and, in particular, after World War II. These agencies required unit and lot evaluations that favored the financing of new suburban houses, thereby encouraging out-migration from central cities to suburbs. They also used neighborhood racial composition as a standard for evaluating the suitability of loans and redlined African American neighborhoods. Combining these criteria, the agencies awarded very few loans to predominantly African American areas, and most FHA and VA home financing went to white suburban communities. Additionally, real estate blockbusting ensured that inner-city neighborhoods rapidly turned from white to black (Gotham 2002a, 2000b; Hirsch 1983; Orser 1994; Seligman 2005). Kevin Gotham (2002a, 97; see also Gotham 2002b) shows poignantly how real estate agents in Kansas City, Missouri, used unscrupulous scare tactics to encourage whites to move out of neighborhoods because " 'the black race was moving in,' " whether such in-movement of blacks was occurring or not. These actions produced rapid turnover from white to black because they instilled fear among whites regarding falling property values and rising crime. Such "blockbusting" was highly profitable for realtors who encouraged whites to sell at low prices and then offered these same units to African American households at higher prices (Hirsch 1983; Orser 1994; Seligman 2005).

Although these types of practices are now illegal, discriminatory actions that help to maintain segregated residential patterns persist (Bond and Williams 2007; Pager and Shepherd 2008; Ross and Turner 2005; Ross and Yinger 2002; Squires and Kubrin 2006). These practices include: African Americans and other nonwhites receiving less information than whites about available housing; nonwhite and white renters and homebuyers being steered to neighborhoods with racial compositions that reflect their own race or ethnicity; and persistent discrimination in mortgage lending (such as higher rates of interest, more loan denials, and greater use of subprime loans for minorities than for whites). The most direct evidence of housing discrimination comes from large audit studies conducted by the U.S. Department of Housing and Urban Development (HUD) in 1989 and 2000 (Ross and Turner 2005; Yinger 1995). The audit methodology involves sending pairs of matched white-black and white-Latino individuals to respond to newspaper advertisements for housing units for rent or sale and then assessing the differential treatment of "comparable" individuals. Housing discrimination against African Americans declined between 1989 and 2000. However, African Americans still received worse treatment than whites in the various stages of a housing search. Perhaps most alarming were dramatic increases in racial steering for African Americans. By comparison, discrimination against Latinos did not decline appreciably between 1989 and 2000. And indeed, Latinos experienced more negative treatment than whites in renting housing throughout the period. Of additional importance was a rise in the withholding of advice and assistance from this group in obtaining the financing required to purchase a home (Ross and Turner 2005).

Racial differentials in mortgage denial and interest rates, as well as dramatic increases in subprime and manufactured housing (in other words, "mobile homes") from the 1990s on have also been documented (Krivo and Kaufman 2004; Oliver and Shapiro 2006; Ross and Yinger 2002; Williams, Nesiba, and McConnell 2005). African Americans and Latinos are much more likely than comparable whites to have their mortgage applications denied, and when approved, they are charged higher interest rates (Krivo and Kaufman 2004; Oliver and Shapiro 2006; Williams et al. 2005). In addition, growth in the risky subprime and manufactured housing loan markets since the early 1990s has been especially great for African Americans at all income levels and for households in nonwhite neighborhoods (Squires and Kubrin 2006; Williams et al. 2005). While increases in conventional home lending lead to reductions in segregation, the expansion of specialized high-risk lending has either no such effect or in fact the opposite effect (Bond and Williams 2007). Thus, shifts in the nature of mortgage markets over the last decade and a half have both reinforced and increased black-white metropolitan segregation.[7]

Differences in the value and appreciation of housing across groups and neighborhoods of different colors also contribute to the persistence of residential segregation. Chenoa Flippen (2004) demonstrates that housing values appreciate more slowly in neighborhoods where the African American population is large or where it grows rapidly after homes are purchased. A high concentration of Latino residents also substantially reduces housing appreciation. Indeed, "the lower appreciation of minority-owned homes costs them literally tens of thousands of dollars in housing equity, the adverse effects of which accumulate over the life course and contribute to the dramatically lower asset accumulation of minority families" (Flippen 2004, 1545). These negative economic costs of living in minority neighborhoods reinforce patterns of segregation over the short and long run. Dramatically reduced housing wealth among African Americans and Latinos limits their abilities to move to white areas, where housing is more expensive (Shapiro 2004).

The persistence of white racist attitudes provides another leg supporting continued racial residential segregation (see Bobo and Zubrinsky 1996; Charles 2003, 2006; Krysan and Bader 2007; Krysan, Farley, and Couper 2008). For example, Camille Charles (2000, 2003, 2006, 2007) shows that there is an unquestionable racial hierarchy of residential preferences in which all nonblack groups (not just non-Hispanic whites) view blacks as their least desired neighbors. Racial stereotyping reduces openness to integration with other groups and increases the desire for same-race neighbors. These relationships are most pronounced for whites (Bobo and Zubrinsky 1996; Charles 2000, 2003). Furthermore, in *Won't You Be My Neighbor* (2006) Charles provides critical empirical evidence that these attitudes matter; individuals who have a stronger preference for integration, whether they are white, black, Latino, or Asian, actually live in neighborhoods with more out-group members.[8] Maria Krysan, Reynolds Farley, and Mick Couper (2008, 7) conclude that "race—and a desire to avoid living with African Americans—continues to shape Whites' perceptions about housing options" in ways that support the persistence of racial residential segregation (see also Farley, Couper, and Krysan 2007; Farley et al. 1978; Farley et al. 1994; Krysan 2002a, 2002b; Krysan and Bader 2007). In videotaped experiments conducted in neighborhoods of varying social classes, Krysan, Farley, and Couper (2008) found that whites rate identical-looking areas as having lower-quality schools and being significantly less expensive, less safe, and less likely to appreciate in value when blacks are shown there compared to when only whites are represented. Where whites would consider living is also strongly associated with the presence of more whites, and such households are particularly resistant to residing in areas where they are not the overwhelming majority (Krysan and Bader 2007).

The variety of practices described here are heavily responsible for the dramatic levels of residential separation of whites and African Americans and the modest levels of segregation of whites from both Latinos and Asians (see, for example, Logan, Stults, and Farley 2004; Massey and Denton 1993; Wilkes and Iceland 2004). In the average metropolitan area in 2000, nearly two-thirds (65.2 percent) of African Americans (or whites) would have to move to a different neighborhood to achieve an even residential distribution—that is, one in which every neighborhood has the same percentage of African Americans and whites as in the entire metropolitan area (Logan, Stults, and Farley 2004). Further, nearly 70 percent of metropolitan blacks live in areas that fall in the high range of segregation. Although still high, black-white segregation has steadily declined since at least 1980, when over 73 percent of blacks (or whites) would have had to move to a different neighborhood to achieve perfect integration.[9] Of note, the largest decreases have been in metropolitan areas with small black populations, where the potential for white contact with African Americans is modest (Krivo and Kaufman 1999; Logan et al. 2004).

The residential segregation of Latinos and Asians from whites is less dramatic and has changed little over the years. In 2000 just over half (51.6 percent) of Latinos and more than two-fifths (44.2 percent) of Asians would have had to change neighborhoods to achieve residential evenness with whites (Logan et al. 2004); these average segregation levels were nearly identical to those of two decades earlier. Stability in segregation for Latinos and Asians apparently stems from the large influx of immigrants into the United States from Central America, South America, the Caribbean, and many parts of Asia since 1965 (for support for this pattern for Latinos, see Logan et al. 2004). New immigrants often move into communities where persons from their country of origin have already settled (Alba and Nee 2003; Massey et al. 1987; Portes and Rumbaut 1996; Zavodny 1999; but see, for example, the discussion of newer settlement patterns in Light and von Scheven 2008). The continuing flow of in-migrants maintains segregation for the Latino and Asian populations as a whole, even while longer-term immigrants and individuals from later generations move away from ethnic concentrations (Iceland 2009; Rosenbaum and Friedman 2007).

Why is the persistence of racial and ethnic residential segregation in the United States so critical to the maintenance and reproduction of a racialized hierarchy of the neighborhood conditions that ultimately lead to crime? One answer lies in how neighborhoods provide residents with access (or the lack thereof) to a wide range of important social and institutional resources (see, for example, Logan and Molotch 1987) and the extent to which separate is still not equal more than fifty years after the overturning of *Plessy v. Ferguson* (Carr and Kutty 2008; Massey and Denton 1993).[10] These resources include schools, political representation, many government services, housing wealth, and local businesses that provide jobs, goods, and services. A couple of examples will suffice to illustrate how these important neighborhood resources are inequitably distributed across communities of different colors in the United States. The tight connection between residential location and where children attend school is often in the forefront of decisions about where to live. The wide variance in the physical and academic quality of schools is closely connected to the economic and racial composition of areas (Reskin 2004; Roscigno 1998; Solorzano and Ornelas 2002). Differences are especially large across school districts (Grant-Thomas and powell 2009; McKoy and Vincent 2008; powell 2007), and parents with resources are willing to pay higher housing prices for access to schools with higher test scores and school ratings (Black 1999; Figlio and Lucas 2002). There may also be significant gaps in expenditures across elementary schools *within the same school district* depending on the poverty and minority composition of students (Condron and Roscigno 2003). In short, the connection between the whiteness of the student body and school quality is strong in the minds of white parents and dramatically influences where they choose to live (Johnson and Shapiro 2003; Shapiro 2004).

As a second example, within a racially structured society a range of organizations, such as businesses and lending agencies, make decisions about where to invest—or disinvest—partially based on the racial composition of neighborhoods. Predominantly white areas often receive more—and more highly valued—economic and social investments, while nonwhite communities are more likely to be neglected or targeted for disinvestments or placement of disruptive institutions (Squires and Kubrin 2006; Squires and O'Connor 2001; Vélez 2006). Elvin Wyly and Steven Holloway (1999) report that, during the 1990s, middle-income white neighborhoods in Atlanta received more than four times as many home loans as middle-income black neighborhoods and that the total dollar amount of these loans was more than five and a half times greater for white areas than for black areas. Large public housing projects (and current forms of subsidized housing redevelopment) are disproportionately sited in disadvantaged neighborhoods and almost exclusively in African American communities (Hirsch 1983; Massey and Denton 1993; Massey and Kanaiaupuni 1993; Pattillo 2007). Deborah Wallace and Roderick Wallace (2001) describe substantial acts of disinvestment in New York's "planned shrinkage" of firehouses during the 1970s, which destroyed large segments of property in poor African American and Puerto Rican areas. Such acts are not relics of a bygone era. For example, New York City recently approved Columbia University's plan to expand high-end development into Harlem, which will bring new affluence into this neighborhood but leave untouched much of the public and low-income housing and impoverishment found in portions of this area (Beveridge 2008; see also Freeman 2006).

Another reason why segregation helps to maintain racially stratified neighborhoods lies in how it concentrates the inequalities produced in and by other institutions into racially distinct communities of privilege or disadvantage (Jargowsky 1997; Krivo et al. 1998; Massey and Denton 1993; Massey and Eggers 1990; Massey and Fischer 2000). Under conditions of residential segregation, the racial and ethnic differences in income and poverty that emanate from the labor market produce large differences in the economic status of white, African American, and other ethno-racial neighborhoods (Massey and Denton 1993). In particular, segregation concentrates white advantages within white neighborhoods. Conversely, African American areas are mired in multiple disadvantages because segregation concentrates the higher levels of African American poverty, joblessness, and the like within predominantly black neighborhoods. With more modest segregation, levels of disadvantage in neighborhoods of other colors reflect the positions of such groups in the social hierarchy—most often between blacks and whites.

Research confirms the connection between segregation and the concentration of poverty and other disadvantages within particular neighborhoods for blacks and other nonwhite populations (Jargowsky 1997; Krivo et al. 1998; Massey and Denton 1993; Massey and Eggers 1990; Massey and Fischer 2000). Thus, for metropolitan areas in 1980 and 1990, poverty rates for African Americans, Asians, and Latinos were all more highly concentrated in places that were more segregated (Jargowsky 1997; Massey and Eggers 1990; Massey and Fischer 2000). Greater segregation also leads to a heightened concentration of African American levels of female-headed families and jobless males (Krivo et al. 1998; but see Quillian 2003). Racial segregation's influence on white-concentrated disadvantage is strikingly different: it generally has no effect and can even benefit this group by reducing the concentration of poverty and female-headed families. Further, racial residential segregation increases the concentration of white affluence (St. John 2002).

In sum, within the United States there is a clear *racial-spatial divide.* By this we mean a social arrangement in which substantial ethno-racial inequality in social and economic circumstances and power in society is combined with segregated and unequal residential locations across major racial and ethnic groups. This racial-spatial divide is hierarchical, with whites in the most advantaged and powerful positions and African Americans in the most disadvantaged and least powerful positions. Other groups, including Latinos and Asians, occupy varying and perhaps more fluid positions in between the two sides of this divide (see, for example, Bonilla-Silva and Glover 2004). As a whole, this socio-spatial organization provides a significant structural mechanism that imprints inequality across groups in local settings that are critical contexts for social action. The racial-spatial divide also provides visible signals to those who manage institutions and resources about the relative value and risks associated with locating in different neighborhoods in an urban area. Although these signals reflect both racial composition and nonracial factors (for example, levels of poverty or street disorder), the racial-spatial divide ensures that ultimately decisions about where to locate or invest will map onto the racially segregated geographic landscape. As such, racial-spatial inequality is created and re-created in a self-reinforcing manner. The dramatically racialized structural circumstances of the racial-spatial divide provide the context for ethno-racial inequality in crime across neighborhoods. In the following sections, we outline specifically how differentials in structural context set the stage for such neighborhood differences in crime.

The Racial-Spatial Divide and Crime

How do racialized neighborhood patterns that are supported through segregation connect with racial and ethnic differences in levels of crime? The racial-spatial divide uniquely situates neighborhoods with distinct ethno-racial compositions in terms of the local conditions that encourage (or discourage) and control (or fail to control) crime (Anderson 1990, 1999; Browning, Feinberg, and Dietz 2004; Krivo and Peterson 1996; Peterson, Krivo, and Browning 2006; Sampson, Raudenbush, and Earls 1997; Sampson and Wilson 1995; Shaw and McKay 1969; Wilson 1987, 1996). Disadvantage is the local condition that is most starkly differentiated by the predominant color of residents. This characteristic is also at the core of social disorganization arguments regarding the role of local structural sources of crime (Shaw and McKay 1969) and is one of the strongest and most consistent predictors of aggregate criminal involvement (Peterson and Krivo 2005; Pratt and Cullen 2005).

Neighborhoods that are highly disadvantaged have heightened crime rates for two broad reasons. First, processes that encourage criminal behavior are particularly prevalent in areas where disadvantage abounds (see, for example, Anderson 1990, 1999; Krivo and Peterson 1996; Peterson, Krivo, and Browning 2006; Sampson and Wilson 1995; Wilson 1987, 1996). Within a context of limited opportunities, theft and other property crimes may occur in an effort to secure resources and luxuries that are not otherwise attainable. Activities such as prostitution, drug trafficking, shoplifting, theft and sale of stolen property, and other opportunistic crimes may become regular sources of "income" and a means of acquiring wanted goods and services (Baskin and Sommers 1998; Venkatesh 2006).[11] Violence as "self-help" may also be used in these crimes, or in other social situations where conflict arises, as participants seek to protect themselves and their possessions rather than engage the police or other authorities (Black 1983; Carr, Napolitano, and Keating 2007; de Haan and Nijboer 2005; Goffman 2009; Jones 2009; Miller 2008; Topalli, Wright, and Fornango 2002; Venkatesh 2006; Wilkinson, Beaty, and Lurry 2009).

As a result of these processes, crime becomes a relatively common aspect of everyday life in more highly disadvantaged communities. As such, residents may be socialized to engage in criminal activity through modeling the actions of others (Anderson 1990, 1999; Krivo and Peterson 1996; Peterson, Krivo, and Browning 2006; Sampson and Wilson 1995; Wilkinson 2003). They witness more illegal behavior and have a greater number of role models who do not restrain their criminal "impulses" or their anger and frustration. The need to adapt to the heightened possibility of criminal victimization and violent encounters often requires that residents be ready, or appear to be ready, to use violence to defend their lives and property. As more people adopt defensive and threatening postures and behaviors such as carrying weapons, the use of violence for defensive purposes increases (Massey 1995). Widespread joblessness and irregular employment may intensify the influence of role modeling and adaptation processes. Many who reside in disadvantaged neighborhoods are idle for much of the day. Idle individuals may spend significant amounts of time in settings where unconventional role modeling and defensive posturing are reactively prevalent—in local taverns and pool halls or on street corners. They are involved in "situations of company" that may be conducive to property crime and violence (Crutchfield 1989; Crutchfield, Matsueda, and Drakulich 2006).

Second, more highly disadvantaged neighborhoods also have more crime because the mechanisms of social control that normally discourage criminal involvement are especially lacking in such contexts. Social control can be difficult to achieve at both the informal and formal levels. Informally, and consistent with social disorganization perspectives, highly disadvantaged communities have more trouble than advantaged areas in organizing to promote common goals, and this undermines their abilities to control crime (see, for example, Browning, Feinberg, and Dietz 2004; Sampson, Raudenbush, and Earls 1997; Shaw and McKay 1969). For example, neighbors may be less likely to serve as eyes and ears for one another, to supervise one another's children, or to act collectively in response to trouble in the neighborhood. In this event, efforts to prevent and respond to crime would be less effective. Further, such areas are characterized by a high degree of social isolation from mainstream society (Krivo and Peterson 1996; Peterson, Krivo, and Browning 2006; Wilson 1987, 1996). As a consequence, residents have less exposure to conventional role models and are less likely to have jobs. There are fewer "old heads" who provide lessons in staying away from crime and out of trouble, and those who remain no longer have prestige and credibility (Anderson 1990, 1999; Wilkinson 2003). Disadvantaged neighborhoods also have relatively few working- and middle-class families to serve as social buffers cushioning the effects of uneven and poor economic conditions (Wilson 1987, 1996). This impedes the ability of communities to sustain basic institutional structures and various sources of social control (Carr 2005; Peterson, Krivo, and Harris 2000; Small and McDermott 2006; Wilson 1987, 1996).

Formally, diminished social control may result from ineffective police protection. At times this is evident in an insufficient supply and deployment of officers, failure to respond to calls from residents, or slow and irregular responses. In impoverished nonwhite communities, policing is also ineffective because it is (or is believed to be) racialized or even harmful (see, for example, Carr, Napolitano, and Keating 2007; Goffman 2009; Jones 2009; Miller 2008; Solis, Portillos, and Brunson 2009; Weitzer and Tuch 2006; Wilkinson, Beaty, and Lurry 2009). Thus, residents are unwilling to ask police to resolve disputes or address victimization. As a result, the costs associated with engaging in crime are lessened and the possible deterrent effect of the law is reduced. In short, residents of disadvantaged communities lack adequate financial, social, and institutional resources to effectively prevent and fight crime (see, for example, Bursik and Grasmick 1993).

Disadvantage is not the only neighborhood factor that affects local crime rates. Levels of residential instability, rates of external investment, and the degree of immigrant concentration are also important. According to social disorganization theory, greater residential instability increases crime by undermining social control (Kornhauser 1978; Sampson, Raudenbush, and Earls 1997). Residents of more unstable communities find it difficult to develop common values and realize common goals. High population turnover inhibits the formation of social networks and weakens attachments to local communities. This hinders efforts to mobilize local residents to provide informal social control of neighborhood life (see, for example, Sampson, Raudenbush, and Earls 1997; Shaw and McKay 1969). However, greater stability is not always associated with greater informal social control. In the wake of deindustrialization, many residents fled some of the worst, and often African American, inner-city areas (Beveridge 2008; Jargowsky 1997; Price-Spratlen and Guest 2002; Wilson 1987). As a result, the poor and others constrained from moving are left behind in communities that now see little change in their residents. This *entrenched* stability may signal weaker rather than stronger social organization, making it difficult for residents to work together to control crime.

As noted in the previous section, outside agents respond in distinct ways to varying communities of color: external investors favor white neighborhoods and often neglect African American and other nonwhite areas. Communities that receive sizable investments have good housing, an array of social services, and economic infrastructures that provide opportunities and resources that serve to prevent crime. Substantial outside investments also signal that communities have powerful political and economic connections that they can draw on to bring in resources to fight crime and other threats (Squires and Kubrin 2006; Vélez 2001, 2006). In contrast, a relative absence of external investments creates major challenges for an area's physical appearance and institutional viability. Such communities have difficulty repairing dilapidated housing, recruiting home buyers, sustaining existing businesses, and attracting new businesses. As a result, physical deterioration and disorder, both of which have been linked to crime, continue unchecked (Kelling and Coles 1996; Skogan 1990; see also Sampson and Raudenbush 1999; Taylor 2001). Further, limited outside investments may increase criminogenic conditions such as poor economic opportunities, weak local social ties, and deteriorated community institutions like schools and churches (Taylor 2001).

The prevalence of immigrants is another condition that varies substantially across ethno-racially distinct neighborhoods and is relevant to crime. Historically, scholars have argued that immigration *contributes* to crime and violence by bringing to areas a cultural diversity that makes communication and the sharing of common goals difficult (Martinez 2006; Shaw and McKay 1969). This factor, coupled with limited resources, has been expected to weaken community organization and the ability of residents to work together to control crime. Yet recent studies challenge this contention by demonstrating consistently *lower* rates of violent crime in communities with more immigrants (Lee, Martinez, and Rosenfeld 2001; Martinez 2002; Sampson 2008; Vélez 2006). The exact reasons for this relationship are not fully understood. However, immigrant communities can provide in-group connections and support ethnically based institutions that together integrate residents and counter otherwise common social problems in resource-poor environments. Ramiro Martinez (2002) also argues that Latino and immigrant communities have relatively high levels of labor market attachment (albeit employment in menial jobs), a factor that should reduce involvement in crime (see also Vélez 2006). Further, residents may use their countries of origin as frames of reference in evaluating their life circumstances: as deprived as conditions may be in U.S. barrios and other immigrant areas, conditions may be even worse in their home countries. This point of comparison could counteract the higher crime that might result if immigrants compared their circumstances to those of other populations in the United States (Blau and Blau 1982; Messner and Rosenfeld 2001).

Considerable research shows clear links of disadvantage, residential instability, and immigration with neighborhood crime (Browning, Feinberg, and Dietz 2004; Krivo and Peterson 1996; Morenoff, Sampson, and Raudenbush 2001; Sampson, Raudenbush, and Earls 1997; Shaw and McKay 1969; see also reviews by Peterson and Krivo 2005; Pratt and Cullen 2005; Sampson 2006). Yet this work has some important limitations. First, the role of community investments has received little empirical attention (but see Squires and Kubrin 2006; Vélez 2001, 2006); we do not know whether such investments actually reduce crime. Second, research has seldom explored the connections between glaring divergence in local conditions and crime across communities of distinct colors (for exceptions for criminal violence, see Crutchfield, Matsueda, and Drakulich 2006; Krivo and Peterson 1996; McNulty 2001). It is therefore unclear whether and how race, place, and crime are linked in contemporary urban areas. Third, analysts have not examined and interpreted differential patterns of crime in terms of the deeply embedded racial and ethnic histories of privilege and oppression that create and re-create neighborhood inequality. This is a fundamental problem for attempts to provide a sound explanation of ethno-racial criminal inequality because the racialized reality of neighborhood structures is not a matter of neutral happenstance. Instead, this reality is intricately embedded within much broader forces of social organization that are structured by race and class. Considering the racial-spatial divide as a core concept for organizing and interpreting our analyses provides a more in-depth and meaningful understanding of ethno-racial disparities in crime than heretofore available (see also Peterson and Krivo 2009a).

The City Context of Neighborhood Crime

Neighborhood crime is unquestionably affected by the internal character of areas. However, local communities are embedded in distinct city settings that also have implications for crime. Consider two neighborhoods that are equally disadvantaged and similar in other important ways, such as the level of residential instability. One is located in Chicago and the other in Houston, cities that are quite distinct from one another. Chicago is more highly segregated and more socioeconomically disadvantaged than Houston. Because both of these city characteristics are associated with heightened crime, neighborhoods with the same levels of disadvantage should have more crime if located in Chicago than in Houston.

We consider citywide segregation and socioeconomic disadvantage along with the urban macroeconomic character as three city conditions that are relevant for understanding neighborhood crime overall and across communities of different colors. We have already described how racial residential segregation affects the neighborhood conditions that are more directly related to crime. Here we explicate how the overall extent of segregation for a city may influence neighborhood crime beyond its contribution to conditions within local areas of the city. When groups are residentially segregated from one another, they do not share common local interests and are less likely to work together to solve community problems (Krivo, Peterson, and Kuhl 2009). Historically, white ethnic groups have rarely been segregated from one another to the extent that contemporary African Americans are separated from other groups (Massey and Denton 1993). For example, ostensibly Italian or Jewish neighborhoods contained a mix of different ethnicities that together benefited from efforts to garner political, social, and economic resources. Such common interests are lacking in today's ethno-racial context: with high levels of black-white segregation, it is uncommon for members of these groups to share local residential space. Rather, "the geographic isolation of blacks . . . force[s] nearly all issues to cleave along racial lines" (Massey and Denton 1993, 155). The result is racial and spatial divisions that undermine both the motivation and the coalitions necessary to implement strategies to improve the social and institutional structures that affect crime. Because the segregation of Latinos from whites is not as great as it is for African Americans (Iceland 2009; Logan, Stults, and Farley 2004; Massey and Denton 1993), Latinos are more likely to share space with whites and to have common interests from which to work. As such, the segregation of Latinos may be less consequential for neighborhood crime.

Segregation may also intensify the impact of different views on causes and solutions to crime problems. For instance, African Americans are likely to view crime as resulting from factors such as limited opportunities and discrimination (Bobo and Johnson 2004; Young 1991) and to support structural solutions like economic investments and government programs to rectify these problems. By contrast, whites tend to view crime as stemming from the choices and propensities of individuals and thus favor dealing with it through efforts that foster individual deterrence and incapacitation via incarceration (Bobo and Johnson 2004; Gilliam and Iyengar 2000; Gilliam, Valentino, and Beckmann 2002; Hurwitz and Peffley 1997; Young 1991). In a segregated context, these very different worldviews on what is responsible for crime may make it difficult for whites and blacks to respond collectively to this problem. It may be especially difficult for whites to consider expending scarce resources to address the broad structural underpinnings of urban crime, such as joblessness and poverty.

Finally, in highly segregated cities substantial portions of the population may be detached from social institutions or may view certain institutions (including criminal justice agencies) as illegitimate (Hagan et al. 1998; Hagan, Shedd, and Payne 2005). Broad detachment and high levels of perceived illegitimacy could contribute to crime by creating a general disregard for the law, undermining citizen cooperation in crime control, promoting crime as a form of self-help, and contributing to a lawless atmosphere (LaFree 1998; Messner and Rosenfeld 2001; Rosenfeld 2002; Tyler and Huo 2002).

City-level macroeconomic conditions also contribute to crime throughout an urban area. Characteristics such as the types of jobs available and the level of socioeconomic disadvantage in a city may influence urban neighborhood crime rates. These relationships may be indirect, as when city conditions affect neighborhood crime through their impact on community resources and other local social conditions. For example, employment opportunities affect distributions of income, poverty, unemployment, and workers with unstable secondary-sector jobs within neighborhoods, and these types of disadvantage have been linked to crime (Crutchfield 1989; Crutchfield, Glusker, and Bridges 1999; Crutchfield, Matsueda, and Drakulich 2006; Krivo and Peterson 2004; Parker 2004; Peterson and Krivo 2005; Pratt and Cullen 2005).

Over and above these indirect influences is the potentially direct impact on crime rates of the macroeconomic character of the city in which neighborhoods are located. William Julius Wilson (1987, 1996, 2009) has brought considerable attention to the ways in which deindustrialization, the movement of employment to the South and the West, and the shifting of much manufacturing abroad have harmed the economic and social bases of many urban areas. These transformations have led to large declines in well-paid, stable manufacturing jobs and to substantial increases in poor and otherwise disadvantaged populations in some cities (Parker 2008; Wilson 1987). Places with a small manufacturing base and large economically disadvantaged populations have a weak foundation for supporting a wide array of the beneficial governmental services for neighborhoods that would help to prevent or combat institutional decay, physical and social disorder, and other conditions that underlie crime. They have fewer police resources for prevention and enforcement activities; less support for local programming, such as recreation centers to provide alternative activities for youth who would otherwise "hang out" in situations of company conducive to crime; and fewer services that reduce the signs of physical disorder, such as litter, poor lighting, and abandoned property, that signal that a neighborhood is not in anyone's control (Kelling and Coles 1996; Skogan 1990). Private entities also have fewer resources to invest in the development efforts of local communities and less reason to believe that their efforts would pay off. Thus, the very assets that should contribute to safer neighborhood environments by shoring up the physical and social infrastructure that helps keep crime at bay are absent.

The National Neighborhood Crime Study

The racial-spatial divide described in this chapter presents considerable challenges for evaluating the connections between neighborhood structural conditions, ethno-racial composition, and crime. Because social conditions are typically very dissimilar for white, African American,

Latino, and other neighborhoods, aspects of community context overlap substantially with race-ethnic composition. As a result, it is difficult to compile data and analyze appropriately whether ethno-racial inequality in neighborhood crime is a product of highly divergent local conditions, as we argue, or instead is due to unmeasured differences associated with racial composition. To deal with this problem, researchers must examine neighborhoods that are racially and ethnically distinct but relatively similar in socioeconomic and other conditions. Such an investigation is not straightforward, however, because there are few highly impoverished and otherwise disadvantaged white urban neighborhoods, particularly ones that are as disadvantaged as many African American communities in the United States. Nor are there very many African American neighborhoods that are as affluent and highly advantaged as is common for white areas (Krivo and Peterson 1996; McNulty 2001; Sampson 2009; Sampson, Sharkey, and Raudenbush 2008; Sampson and Wilson 1995).

Two recent studies of Chicago highlight the substantive and methodological problems that stem from U.S. racial neighborhood stratification (Sampson 2009; Sampson, Sharkey, and Raudenbush 2008). Robert Sampson (2009) compared per capita income distributions for white and black neighborhoods in Chicago in 2000. He showed that not a single predominantly white neighborhood had an income level as low as that in the typical black community. Conversely, only a very small proportion of Chicago's African American neighborhoods had per capita income levels as high as those for any white area. This is an important finding because it reflects the significantly racialized structures that we discuss in this book. It also illustrates the problem of analyzing the outcomes of ethno-racial neighborhood inequality within a single city where comparably situated white and African American neighborhoods are virtually nonexistent. As Sampson (2009, 265) notes, "Trying to estimate the effect of concentrated disadvantage on whites is . . . tantamount to estimating a phantom reality." In light of this problem, Robert Sampson, Patrick Sharkey, and Stephen Raudenbush (2008) limit their analysis of the role of concentrated disadvantage in the verbal ability of Chicago children to black youth, because no white children in their sample lived in highly disadvantaged neighborhoods (the top quarter of the distribution for Chicago). Thus, racial-ethnic inequality in outcomes could not be examined.[12]

We conducted the National Neighborhood Crime Study (NNCS) to address this comparability problem by assembling neighborhood crime and other social data for a broad range of cities across the country (Peterson and Krivo 2010). By including local areas in numerous cities, we obtained a sample with a sufficient number of racially and ethnically distinct, but otherwise comparable, neighborhoods to address the linkages of interest. The NNCS is the only study that includes this type of sample.

Crime data were obtained directly from police departments because the central repository of crime information in the United States, the Federal Bureau of Investigation's (FBI) Uniform Crime Reporting (UCR) program, provides data only for entire agencies such as cities, counties, or similar units. The FBI does not collect data for smaller areas within jurisdictions, such as neighborhoods. Prior to the NNCS, studies of neighborhood crime relied on reported violations for a single city or a small number of cities (see, for example, Crutchfield, Matsueda, and Drakulich 2006; Krivo and Peterson 1996; Kubrin and Wadsworth 2003; Lee, Martinez, and Rosenfeld 2001; Martinez, Stowell, and Cancino 2008; McNulty 2001; Morenoff, Sampson, and Raudenbush 2001; Nielsen, Lee, and Martinez 2005; Shihadeh and Shrum 2004; Wooldredge and Thistlethwaite 2003). John Hipp's (2007) study of crime for neighborhoods based on a convenience sample of nineteen cities is the sole exception. These types of samples have limited our ability to explore the role of the U.S. racialized residential landscape in generating crime. In addition, these small- and convenience-sample studies have helped us understand the structural sources of crime in a few cities such as Atlanta, Chicago, Columbus (Ohio), and Seattle, but they tell us little about whether the patterns identified for these places generally hold for U.S. urban areas.

The NNCS includes reported crime counts obtained from police departments and detailed sociodemographic data from the U.S. census and other published sources for 9,593 census tracts—that is, neighborhoods—within a representative sample of 91 large U.S. cities (central cities and suburbs with populations over 100,000) for 2000.[13] The sample of cities was selected from all incorporated places with a population of at least 100,000 in 1999.[14] Cities were chosen randomly within census regions (the Northeast and Midwest combined, the South, and the West) and are distributed throughout the country, as shown in figure 2.3. We contacted the police department in each selected city to obtain data on reported crime incidents for seven FBI index offenses (homicide, rape, robbery, aggravated assault, burglary, larceny, and motor vehicle theft)[15] for 1999 to 2001 for the census tracts within each jurisdiction.[16] We combined census tract crime counts with data on social and demographic characteristics for each tract and for the cities in which the tracts are located from the 2000 census. The NNCS data include cities and large incorporated suburbs in all regions of the country, both those with a declining economy and those with a healthy economy, and places that vary in their levels of racial residential segregation. The sample is highly representative of large cities (at least 100,000 population). Table 2.1 reports the mean values for the crime rate, black-white residential segregation, poverty, racial composition, and region for the ninety-one cities in the NNCS and for all large U.S. cities for 2000. These data show that for each of the dimensions except

Figure 2.3   Cities in the National Neighborhood Crime Study

Source: ESRI (2006).

region, the NNCS sample cities differ, on average, by at most 10 percent from the population of places with over 100,000 residents. The regional distributions of our sample and of all large U.S. cities are relatively comparable. Our sample slightly overrepresents places in the Northeast and Midwest and somewhat underrepresents cities in the West.

In this book, we examine 8,931 census tracts across 87 cities for which complete information is available for the crimes analyzed. (See table 2A.1 for a list of the cities included.) Given our primary interest in comparing crime patterns across local areas with distinct ethno-racial compositions, we categorize neighborhoods as predominantly white, predominantly African American, predominantly Latino, minority, or integrated. Neighborhoods are defined as predominantly white, African American, or Latino if the respective group constitutes at least 70 percent of the tract population. With these classifications, whites and African Americans include only non-Latinos; Latinos include people who identified with any census racial category.[17] Areas are designated as minority when the combination of African Americans and Latinos makes up 70 percent or more of the population, but neither group alone is more than 70 percent. All other tracts are considered integrated neighborhoods because they have a greater balance of racial and ethnic groups. The sample includes 3,115 white neighborhoods, 1,467 African American neighborhoods, 679 Latino

Table 2.1   Mean Values for Selected Characteristics of U.S. Cities with
Populations over 100,000 and NNCS Sample Cities, 2000

Characteristic	All Large U.S. Cities	NNCS Cities
Index crime rate per 100,000	6,104.4	6,374.5
Black-white segregation	43.9%	47.5%
Poverty rate	15.1	15.4
Percentage white	53.9	54.8
Percentage African American	17.4	18.6
Percentage Latino	19.8	19.1
Region		
Northeast-Midwest	28.2	36.3
South	32.7	35.2
West	39.2	28.6

Source: Authors' calculations based on data from the National Neighborhood Crime Study (Peterson and Krivo 2010), the 2000 census (U.S. Bureau of the Census 2007), Federal Bureau of Investigation (2001), and the Lewis Mumford Center for Comparative Urban and Regional Research (2009).

neighborhoods, 645 minority neighborhoods, and 3,025 integrated neighborhoods. Note that there are almost as many integrated areas as there are predominantly white areas. The group of integrated neighborhoods is also larger than any of the three types of predominantly nonwhite (African American, Latino, or minority) neighborhoods. Readers may be concerned that integrated areas include a "mishmash" of many distinct types of communities. Indeed, such neighborhoods vary in terms of which groups reside together. About 40 percent each are dominated by either African Americans and whites or Latinos and whites; the remainder are more diverse. Despite these differences in population composition, the three types of integrated communities are extremely similar to each other in levels of disadvantage, residential instability, and external investments. They differ, however, in that African American–white areas have a much lower presence of immigrants than all other integrated neighborhoods. There is also variation in crime rates: the most violent crimes and property crimes occur in integrated contexts that have more African Americans. However, the overall pattern of results and the story emanating from the findings about race and crime are essentially the same for the three types of integrated areas as for the combined set.

Measures of Crime and Context

We examine the racialized social context of crime in urban neighborhoods using average annual counts of violent and property crimes reported to the police over the three-year period from 1999 to 2001.

(See table 2A.2 for more detail on definitions of these and all other measures.)[18] Violent crimes include homicide and robbery. Property crimes include burglary, larceny, and motor vehicle theft.[19] As noted, the key neighborhood factors examined are residential instability, residential loans, immigrant prevalence, and socioeconomic disadvantage. The measure of residential instability is an index that combines the prevalence of renters and of residents who moved to the neighborhood recently.[20] The level of residential loans taps external investments into local communities and is measured as the total dollar amount of home loans issued (originated) in the census tract.[21] Immigrant prevalence is an index comprised of the relative size of the foreign-born population, the percentage of recent immigrants to the United States, and the percentage of households that are linguistically isolated (no one speaks English well). Disadvantage combines the prevalence of six neighborhood factors: poverty, joblessness, low-wage jobs, female-headed families, lack of professional workers, and absence of college graduates. We control for the presence of young males in all multivariate analyses because this group is disproportionately involved in crime. Residential loan information is from Home Mortgage Disclosure Act data (Federal Financial Institutions Examination Council 2001). Data for all other social and economic factors are taken from the U.S. census.

Our models of violent and property crime include several contextual characteristics of the cities in which the neighborhoods are located: black-white residential segregation, city disadvantage (measured in a parallel fashion to the neighborhood disadvantage indicator), and the prevalence of manufacturing employment. Racial residential segregation is measured with the widely used Black-White Index of Dissimilarity (D) for census tracts. D measures the extent of deviation from evenness of blacks and whites across areas within each city. It ranges from 0 to 100, with values representing the percentage of blacks (or whites) who would have to change their tract of residence to achieve perfect integration. For example, in Chicago, the most segregated city in our sample, the Index of Dissimilarity is 85.2: just over 85 percent of blacks (or whites) in this city would have to move to a different Chicago neighborhood for the city to become completely integrated. The segregation data were acquired from the Lewis Mumford Center for Comparative Urban and Regional Research (2009).[22]

In addition to the three theoretical conditions, we control for a set of city factors owing to their well-known relationships with crime rates: population size, percentage of African Americans, percentage of recent movers, percentage of foreign-born, percentage of young males, and regional location. In the next chapter, we begin the analysis by describing the extent of residential separation of whites, African Americans, and Latinos in the neighborhoods in the selected U.S. cities and detailing the patterns of differentiation in neighborhood conditions across the five ethno-racial neighborhood types.

Conclusion: The Next Step

In this chapter, we have set the stage for our empirical findings in three ways. First, we made it clear that levels of violent and property crime vary substantially across neighborhoods comprising different race-ethnic groups in urban areas in the United States. This variation reveals a hierarchy in which predominantly white neighborhoods experience by far the least crime and African Americans areas by far the most crime, although this pattern is clearer and more stark for violent crimes than for property offenses. Accounting for these differences is the core goal of this book. Second, we framed our empirical exploration by integrating a broad racialized perspective on society with a criminological approach drawing on social disorganization theory and insights from urban sociology. Our approach holds that inequalities in the social and economic conditions of racial and ethnic groups and their communities are integral parts of a U.S. social order in which whites are privileged at the expense of other groups. This societal organization produces African American, Latino, and other nonwhite neighborhoods that suffer from the host of structural disadvantages that are central to the generation of crime. Thus, differences in rates of crime across neighborhoods of different colors are a critical consequence of a racially stratified society that should be understood in this light. Third, we described the unique data set, the National Neighborhood Crime Study, that we use to explore the racially structured underpinnings of criminal inequality in both violent and property offenses. The unprecedented breadth of the NNCS sample of neighborhoods across cities permits a closer and more accurate look at race, place, and crime than has ever before been possible. In discussing the NNCS, we also outlined how we measure the key factors examined and conduct the analyses that follow.

Having set the stage in these ways, we can now proceed to our four-part empirical tale. The next chapter tells the first two parts of this tale. We begin by describing the residential separation of whites, African Americans, and Latinos. We then proceed to highlight how this separation is connected with dramatic differentiation in the social and economic character of neighborhoods. Taken together, the data presented make very clear the divergent social worlds of racial and ethnic groups in the urban United States.

Appendix

Table 2A.1   Cities Included in the National Neighborhood Crime Study

Akron, Ohio	Louisville, Kentucky
Albuquerque, New Mexico	Madison, Wisconsin
Alexandria, Virginia	McAllen, Texas
Arlington, Texas	Memphis, Tennessee
Aurora, Illinois	Miami, Florida
Austin, Texas	Milwaukee, Wisconsin
Boston, Massachusetts	Minneapolis, Minnesota
Buffalo, New York	Naperville, Illinois
Carrollton, Texas	Nashville, Tennessee
Chandler, Arizona	New Haven, Connecticut
Charlotte, North Carolina	Newport News, Virginia
Chicago, Illinois	Norfolk, Virginia
Chula Vista, California	Oakland, California
Cincinnati, Ohio	Oklahoma City, Oklahoma
Cleveland, Ohio	Ontario, California
Columbus, Ohio	Overland Park, Kansas
Coral Springs, Florida	Pasadena, California
Dallas, Texas	Pasadena, Texas
Dayton, Ohio	Pembroke Pines, Florida
Denver, Colorado	Phoenix, Arizona
Des Moines, Iowa	Pittsburgh, Pennsylvania
Detroit, Michigan	Plano, Texas
Eugene, Oregon	Portland, Oregon
Evansville, Indiana	Rockford, Illinois
Fort Collins, Colorado	San Bernardino, California
Fort Wayne, Indiana	San Diego, California
Fort Worth, Texas	Santa Rosa, California
Fullerton, California	Seattle, Washington
Garden Grove, California	Simi Valley, California
Glendale, Arizona	St. Louis, Missouri
Hampton, Virginia	St. Petersburg, Florida
Hartford, Connecticut	Stamford, Connecticut
Hialeah, Florida	Sterling Heights, Michigan
Houston, Texas	Tampa, Florida
Inglewood, California	Tempe, Arizona
Irving, Texas	Toledo, Ohio
Jacksonville, Florida	Topeka, Kansas
Kansas City, Missouri	Tucson, Arizona
Knoxville, Tennessee	Virginia Beach, Virginia
Lexington, Kentucky	Waco, Texas
Lincoln, Nebraska	Washington, D.C.
Livonia, Michigan	Waterbury, Connecticut
Long Beach, California	Worcester, Massachusetts
Los Angeles, California	

Source: National Neighborhood Crime Study (Peterson and Krivo 2010).

Table 2A.2   Operationalizations of Variables

Variables	Operationalizations
Dependent variable	
Violent crimes	Three-year (1999 to 2001) average number of homicides and robberies per 1,000 tract population
Property crimes	Three-year (1999 to 2001) average number of burglaries, larcenies, and motor vehicle thefts per 1,000 tract population
Independent variables	
Tract level (N = 8,931)	
Neighborhood ethno-racial composition	Dummy variables for type of area
	White neighborhood, 1 = 70% or more non-Latino white (else = 0) (reference)
	African American neighborhood, 1 = 70% or more non-Latino black (else = 0)
	Latino neighborhood, 1 = 70% or more Latino (else = 0)
	Minority neighborhood, 1 = 70% or more Latinos and non-Latino blacks (else = 0)
	Integrated neighborhood, 1 = any other race-ethnic combination (else = 0)
Residential instability (α = .69)	Average of the standard scores for two variables
	Percentage of occupied housing units that are renter-occupied
	Percentage of population age five and over who lived in a different residence in 1995
Residential loans	Total dollar amount of loans issued in 2000 (in thousands of dollars)
Immigrant prevalence (α = .96)	Average of the standard scores of the following three variables
	Percentage of the total population that is foreign-born
	Percentage of the total population that is foreign-born and arrived in the United States in 1990 or later
	Percentage of households in which no one age fourteen or over speaks English well

(Table continues on p. 48.)

Table 2A.2 *Continued*

Variables	Operationalizations
Disadvantage (α = .93)	Average of the standard scores for six variables
	Percentage of population age sixteen to sixty-four who are unemployed or out of the labor force (joblessness)
	Percentage of employed civilian population age sixteen and over working in professional or managerial occupations (reverse-coded in index)
	Percentage of population age twenty-five and over who are college graduates (reverse-coded in index)
	Percentage of households that are female-headed families
	Percentage of employed civilian population age sixteen and over employed in the six occupational categories with the lowest average incomes (low-wage jobs)
	Percentage of population that is below the poverty line
Percentage of young males	Percentage of the population that is male and age fifteen to thirty-four
City level (N = 87)	
Segregation	Index of Dissimilarity across census tracts within the city between non-Hispanic whites and non-Hispanic blacks
Disadvantage (α = .95)	Average of the standard scores for six variables
	Percentage of population age sixteen to sixty-four who are unemployed or out of the labor force (joblessness)

	Percentage of employed civilian population age sixteen and over working in professional or managerial occupations (reverse-coded in index)
	Percentage of population age twenty-five and over who are college graduates (reverse-coded in index)
	Percentage of households that are female-headed families
	Percentage of employed civilian population age sixteen and over employed in the six occupational categories with the lowest average incomes (low-wage jobs)
	Percentage of population that is below the poverty line
Manufacturing jobs	Percentage of employed civilian population age sixteen and over working in a manufacturing industry
Population	Total city population
Percentage African American	Percentage of the population that is non-Latino black
Percentage movers	Percentage of the population age five and over who lived in a different residence in 1995
Percentage foreign-born	Percentage of the population that is foreign-born
Percentage young males	Percentage of the population that is male and age fifteen to thirty-four
South	1 = South (0 if else)
West	1 = West (0 if else)

Source: National Neighborhood Crime Study (Peterson and Krivo 2010).

Chapter 3

Divergent Social Worlds

THE STARK reality of U.S. society is that whites, African Americans, and Latinos live in strikingly different social worlds. These divergent communities of color reflect the entrenched inequalities found in a racially structured society in which whites are highly privileged compared to other populations. Groups of varying colors commonly live in separate residential areas that are far from similar in key social conditions that put communities at peril for, or protect them from, a host of social problems. In this chapter, we provide a portrait of white, African American, Latino, minority, and integrated neighborhoods in large U.S. cities that documents just how different these types of communities are from one another. As we have argued, such differences in social conditions provide the backdrop for crime, one key urban social problem that is highly variable across areas of different colors.

The Distinct Colors of Residence

The separate neighborhoods in which whites, African Americans, and Latinos commonly reside are shown clearly in figure 3.1 for our sample of urban areas. The figure reports the percentage of each group that lives in predominantly white, African American, Latino, minority, or integrated areas. A full 60 percent of whites in the large cities we study live in communities in which their neighbors are mainly (70 percent or more) fellow whites, and half of African Americans reside in areas where most residents are African American. Latinos are less segregated from other groups, but one-third have predominantly Latino neighbors. This level of concentration is especially striking, and far greater than would be randomly expected, in a context where fewer than half of all residents are white and only slightly more than 20 percent are African American or Latino, respectively.

Residential separation into predominantly same-race neighborhoods is greatest for whites, for whom a mere 5 percent live in areas with very large numbers of African Americans or Latinos. However, residential divisions are not limited to those distinguishing whites from nonwhites.

Figure 3.1   Whites, African Americans, and Latinos Living in Each of the Five Ethno-Racial Neighborhood Types

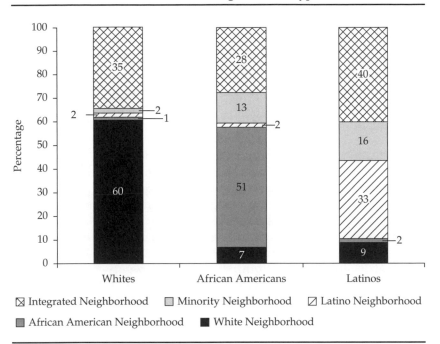

Source: National Neighborhood Crime Study (Peterson and Krivo 2010).

Only 15 percent of African Americans live in neighborhoods with a large representation of Latinos (minority or Latino areas); 18 percent of Latinos live in areas in which African American residents are numerous (minority or African American areas). Although neighborhood ethno-racial segregation is typical for whites and African Americans, notable portions of all three groups live in integrated neighborhoods. More than one-third of whites and one-quarter of African Americans reside in such areas, while 40 percent of Latinos live in integrated neighborhoods.

Nearly forty years ago, the report of the National Advisory Commission on Civil Disorders (1968)—the so-called Kerner Commission Report—warned that we were moving toward two societies, one black and one white. More recently, Massey and Denton (1993, 15) have described the U.S. residential system as an "American apartheid" in which actions and practices systematically isolate African Americans, as happened to South Africans, "within a narrowly circumscribed portion of the urban environment . . . [that] forces blacks to live under extraordinarily harsh conditions." Unlike in South Africa, America's apartheid did not develop exclusively out of prescriptive legal statutes, though legally supported policies and practices such as restrictive covenants, redlining, and the placement of public housing were at the heart of the historical processes that created segregated African American ghettos (Gotham 2002a, 2002b; Haynes 2008; Hirsch 1983; Jackson 1985; Massey and Denton 1993; Orser 1994; Seligman 2005). These deliberate practices existed with the tacit approval of whites. Thus, by 1980, in many metropolitan areas the residential separation of African Americans from whites was so great across multiple dimensions of segregation that Massey and Denton described it as a pattern of hypersegregation. Indeed, sixteen large metropolitan areas that housed one-third of all U.S. African Americans were hypersegregated in 1980.

Massey and Denton analyzed only fifty of the largest metropolitan areas. Since their book *American Apartheid* was published in 1993, other social scientists have updated their analysis and expanded the sample (Denton 1994; Logan, Stults, and Farley 2004; Wilkes and Iceland 2004). These more recent studies show that residential segregation between blacks and whites has declined somewhat since 1980, but still persists at very high levels. In fact, in both 1990 and 2000, twenty-nine metropolitan areas in the United States were hypersegregated. These included places in all regions of the country, although the most extreme levels are found in the Northeast and Midwest. Residential separation from whites is considerably less extensive for Latinos than for African Americans (see, for example, Logan et al. 2004). Only two metropolitan areas showed Latino-white hypersegregation in 2000 (Wilkes and Iceland 2004).

Our data on the overall concentration of the white, African American, and Latino populations in same-race versus other types of neighborhoods provide clear evidence of how general patterns of segregation play out. They do not, however, fully illustrate Massey and Denton's (1993) contention that the urban United States is an American apartheid that presents uniquely high levels of isolation for African Americans. The distinct and extraordinary isolation of African Americans is shown dramatically in figure 3.2, which displays the percentages of each of the three ethno-racial groups living in neighborhoods made up almost completely (more than 90 percent) of residents from the same group. Over one-third of African Americans live in neighborhoods that are almost exclusively African American. A clear majority of whites and a sizable portion of Latinos live in predominantly same-race areas (figure 3.1), but their separation into exclusively single-group-dominated communities is not nearly as extreme as it is for African Americans. Only 14 percent of whites and 9 percent of Latinos reside in areas with over 90 percent of their own group.

If segregation was neutral in its social consequences, the separation of ethno-racial groups into different neighborhoods would not be a critical concern. However, the effects of segregation are by no means neutral. In

Figure 3.2   Whites, African Americans, and Latinos in Neighborhoods with 90 Percent or More of the Same Race-Ethnicity

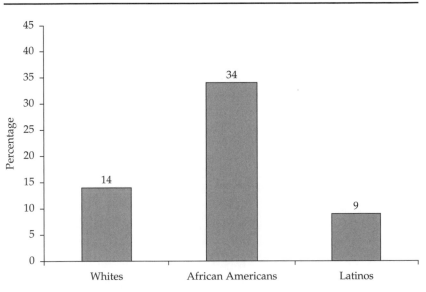

Source: National Neighborhood Crime Study (Peterson and Krivo 2010).

the next section, we turn to a description of just how consequential segregation is in the U.S. racial context.

Ethno-Racial Neighborhood Inequality

Table 3.1 shows the dramatic ethno-racial inequality associated with residential separation for six widely used indicators of social and economic status—poverty, joblessness, low-wage jobs, female-headed families, professional workers, and college graduates. The table presents average levels of these characteristics separately for the white, African American, Latino, minority, and integrated neighborhoods in our study. The results show three overarching patterns of neighborhood differentiation. First, white neighborhoods are especially privileged across all aspects of disadvantage. Fewer than 10 percent of residents of white areas are impoverished, and only about one-quarter of the working-age population lacks a job (either voluntarily or involuntarily).[1] In addition, levels of low-wage employment (12.2 percent) and female headship (8.6 percent) are modest. At the same time, high-status workers and college graduates are prevalent in white communities. Somewhat fewer than half of those who are employed work in high-status jobs, and a full 40 percent of all adults are college graduates.

Table 3.1   Mean Values for Socioeconomic Variables for Neighborhoods of Different Colors

Neighborhood Characteristic	White Areas	African American Areas	Latino Areas	Minority Areas	Integrated Areas
Poverty	8.6%	31.7%	28.9%	28.3%	17.9%
Joblessness	23.5	47.8	47.1	45.0	32.4
Low-wage jobs	12.2	26.3	25.1	25.1	18.4
Female-headed families	8.6	35.7	18.6	24.8	14.7
Professional workers	44.2	21.2	13.1	18.9	31.6
College graduates	39.8	9.9	6.7	10.2	24.4
Number of cases	3,115	1,467	679	645	3,025

Source: National Neighborhood Crime Study (Peterson and Krivo 2010).

Second, there are dramatic consequences for those living in areas with large concentrations of subordinate-group members (African American, Latino, and minority neighborhoods). Average levels of low-status characteristics are generally two to three times higher in the three types of nonwhite neighborhoods (African American, Latino, and minority) compared to white neighborhoods. Almost one-third of residents in the typical African American community are poor. Poverty rates approach this level (approximately 28 percent) in average Latino and minority areas. Even more dramatically, nearly half of the working-age population in the nonwhite areas has no job, and about one-quarter of those who work have positions in the lowest-wage occupations. Reflecting societal differentials in family structure, African American neighborhoods stand out in the high prevalence of female-headed families (36 percent). The two remaining indicators show the opposite side of this portrait. Professional workers are half as common in areas populated by African Americans as in white areas, and there are only one-quarter as many college graduates in the former as in the latter. Latino neighborhoods are even worse off in terms of these two characteristics. Only 13 percent of employed residents work in professional jobs, and a mere 7 percent are college graduates. Minority areas are more similar to African American communities in their average levels of the high-status characteristics.

Third, integrated neighborhoods provide environments that are a combination of those found in white and predominantly nonwhite areas; levels of social and economic characteristics fall between those evident in these two sets of communities. Detrimental conditions are more widespread in integrated neighborhoods than in predominantly white neighborhoods but are notably less prevalent than in African American, Latino, and minority communities. They also have a dearth of high-status individuals when compared to white areas. Yet integrated neighborhoods have substantially more professional workers and college graduates than any of the three types of nonwhite areas.

These comparisons are telling regarding the extent of ethnic and racial neighborhood inequality. However, the values only describe the average point in the distribution for each community condition. They do not indicate whether or how varying levels of the factors overlap, which is a particularly critical concern when we compare neighborhoods of different colors in the United States. For example, African American neighborhoods not only differ from other types of local areas in their typical socioeconomic character, but in many places they also diverge so much from white communities that the most advantaged African American areas are no better off than the typical white neighborhood (Krivo and Peterson 2000; McNulty 2001; Peterson and Krivo 2005; Sampson 2009; Sampson, Sharkey, and Raudenbush 2008; Sampson and Wilson 1995). And "the 'worst' urban neighborhoods in which Whites reside are considerably better off than those of the average Black community" (Sampson and Bean 2006, 12).

Examination of the distributions for each of the socioeconomic characteristics grouped into low, high, and extreme levels for differently colored neighborhoods is instructive. These data show the character of the divergent social worlds in which whites and other groups reside even more strikingly than the averages. In fact, there is very little overlap in the residential conditions of whites and the conditions faced by people living in African American, Latino, and minority neighborhoods. Integrated communities share the advantages of white areas *and* the disadvantages of their nonwhite counterparts. This is the case for all six of the average social conditions described in table 3.1. In figures 3.3 and 3.4, we present these results graphically for two of the disadvantage characteristics, poverty and professional workers, as illustrative of this general pattern. (For the remaining four conditions, see figures 3A.1 to 3A.4.)

Figure 3.3 displays levels of poverty for the five types of neighborhood color. Poverty is categorized into low, high, and extreme levels following a widely used convention in research on poverty concentration: less than 20 percent, 20 to 39 percent, and 40 percent or more (Jargowsky 2003; Jargowsky and Bane 1990, 1991). The results in the figure are stark. Low poverty levels are pervasive in white neighborhoods, with almost all areas (over 90 percent) falling into this category. Further examination of the distribution of white neighborhoods with low poverty reveals that most have rates below 10 percent, and a striking 37 percent have fewer than 5 percent poor residents (results not shown). Extreme poverty characterizes a mere 1 percent of white communities.

The contrast with African American, Latino, and minority neighborhoods could hardly be more extreme. Only about one-quarter of each of

Figure 3.3   Neighborhood Types with Varying Levels of Poverty

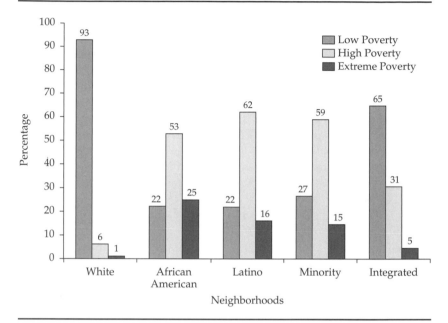

Source: National Neighborhood Crime Study (Peterson and Krivo 2010).

these three types of nonwhite areas has a low poverty rate. For African American areas, a very similar number have extreme poverty as have low poverty. Fewer Latino and minority areas (16 and 15 percent, respectively) than African American neighborhoods (25 percent) have extreme poverty levels. Further, a clear majority of all three nonwhite neighborhood types are highly impoverished. Overall, a paltry 7 percent of white communities are highly or extremely poor, while fully three-quarters of African American, Latino, and minority areas reach these high levels. Integrated neighborhoods are more like white neighborhoods, although poverty is more pervasive there than for the most privileged population in the United States. Nearly two-thirds of integrated areas have low poverty, and only 5 percent are extremely poor. Still, a sizable 31 percent (compared to 6 percent for white areas and well over 50 percent for each of the predominantly nonwhite neighborhoods) fall into the high poverty category.

Figure 3.4 presents the data for the prevalence of workers in professional occupations. Here we again see the unquestionably privileged status of white communities: nearly 60 percent reach the threshold of having many professional workers (40 percent or more), and only 7 percent have few professionals (fewer than 20 percent) living in the area.[2]

Figure 3.4   Neighborhood Types with Varying Levels of Professional Workers

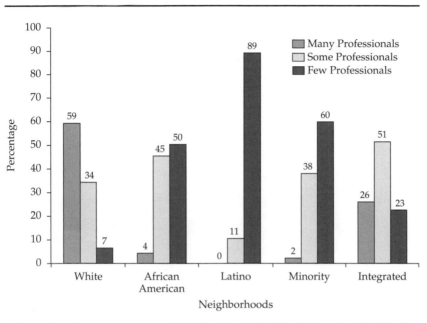

Source: National Neighborhood Crime Study (Peterson and Krivo 2010).

The contrasting patterns for African American, Latino, and minority neighborhoods are pronounced: at most, 4 percent of these communities have a large number of professionals. At the other extreme, half of African American neighborhoods, 60 percent of minority areas, and a whopping 89 percent of Latino neighborhoods are characterized by a low number of high-status workers. The integrated neighborhoods are situated between the levels of this aspect of advantage (or disadvantage) found in white and nonwhite areas.

Constellations of Disadvantage

To this point, we have described the different social worlds found in white, African American, Latino, minority, and integrated neighborhoods for individual dimensions of disadvantage. In reality, however, poverty, joblessness, high-status work, and other conditions do not exist apart from one another. Rather, they overlap, albeit to varying degrees, across ethno-racial groups and local communities. We take this point into account by examining how all six characteristics come together to create contexts of overall disadvantage (or advantage) that vary across neighborhoods.

**Figure 3.5   Disadvantage Distributions for White and
African American Neighborhoods**

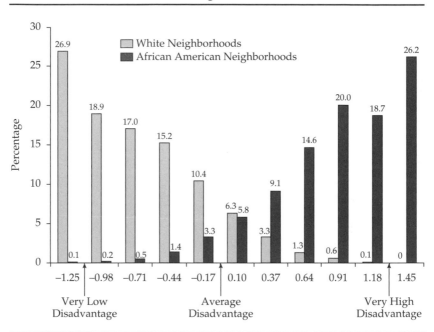

Source: National Neighborhood Crime Study (Peterson and Krivo 2010).
Note: Disadvantage Index values represent the midpoint of equal-size categories.

The portrait drawn when looking at constellations of community conditions reveals that the divergent residential worlds of whites, African Americans, and Latinos are even more distinct than we have already seen.

Figures 3.5 through 3.8 illustrate the comparative disadvantage distributions for white versus African American, white versus Latino, white versus minority, and white versus integrated neighborhoods. Disadvantage is measured for each neighborhood as an index that combines poverty, joblessness, low-wage jobs, female-headed families, nonprofessional workers, and noncollege graduates. A value of 0 on the disadvantage index represents *average* disadvantage relative to the mean for all neighborhoods in the large cities studied here. More negative values (to the left of 0) reflect an increasingly lower prevalence of adverse conditions. As the index becomes more positive (to the right of 0), the values symbolize an ever greater complex of disadvantages.

The white–African American neighborhood comparison shown in figure 3.5 indicates that very few white areas have above-average disadvantage (greater than 0). We find an increasing percentage of white

**Figure 3.6   Disadvantage Distributions for White and
                 Latino Neighborhoods**

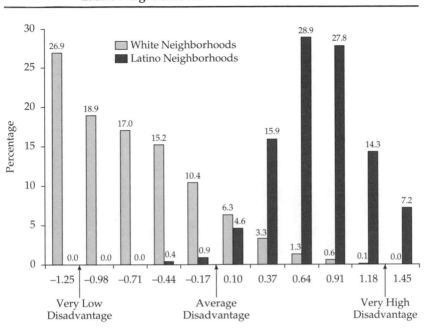

Source: National Neighborhood Crime Study (Peterson and Krivo 2010).
Note: Disadvantage Index values represent the midpoint of equal-size categories.

neighborhoods as we move toward lower and lower levels of disadvantage; over one-quarter of these communities have extremely low levels. African American communities are in the exact opposite situation. Most have above-average disadvantage (greater than 0), and as we move toward the higher end of the disadvantage distribution we generally see an increasing proportion of African American areas. A striking 26 percent of black neighborhoods have the most extreme level of disadvantage. In fact, the figure has a decidedly V-shaped appearance because the largest share of white neighborhoods have very low levels of disadvantage while the largest share of African American neighborhoods have high to extremely high levels of overlapping disadvantages.

Figure 3.6 compares white and Latino communities. As already shown in figure 3.5, white areas have levels of disadvantage that are mainly in the low end of the disadvantage distribution. Conversely, most Latino neighborhoods have above-average disadvantage. Both Latino and African American areas are much more disadvantaged than white communities, but the circumstances of these two nonwhite populations are far

Figure 3.7   Disadvantage Distributions for White and Minority Neighborhoods

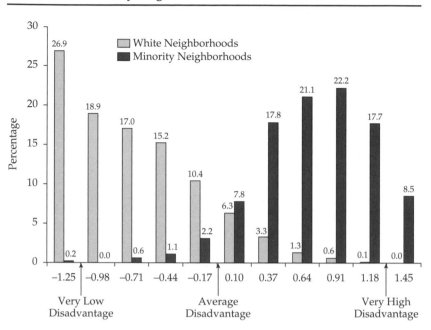

Source: National Neighborhood Crime Study (Peterson and Krivo 2010).
Note: Disadvantage Index values represent the midpoint of equal-size categories.

from identical. (See figure 3A.5 for a direct comparison of the distributions for African American and Latino neighborhoods.) A very large portion of African American neighborhoods are represented at the most extreme disadvantage levels, while Latino communities are heavily clustered at high levels and only modestly represented among extremely disadvantaged levels. At the same time, fewer Latino areas than African American areas are privileged in having below-average levels of the index. A total of 5.5 percent of the African American neighborhoods versus only 1.3 percent of the Latino neighborhoods are in the lowest five categories of disadvantage. Such African American–Latino differences loom large in recent discussions seeking to account for crime rates that are lower in Latino areas than in African American areas. Martinez (2002) and Vélez (2006) point to lower levels of concentrated disadvantage among Latino neighborhoods compared with African American neighborhoods as one possible explanation for this pattern.

Figures 3.7 and 3.8 compare white neighborhoods with minority and integrated areas. The distribution of disadvantage for minority areas is

**Figure 3.8   Disadvantage Distributions for White and
Integrated Neighborhoods**

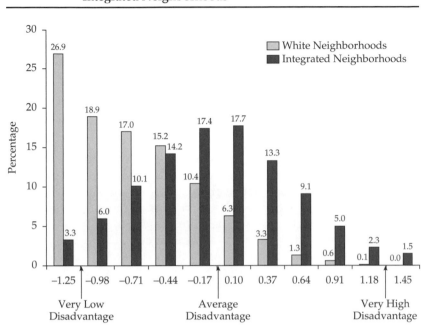

Source: National Neighborhood Crime Study (Peterson and Krivo 2010).
Note: Disadvantage Index values represent the midpoint of equal-size categories.

more similar to those for predominantly African American and Latino
neighborhoods than to that for heavily white areas. The pattern for communities with a substantial mix of the two nonwhite groups reflects the
blending of the populations, with disadvantage concentrated at very
high levels, but not the most extreme levels. Figure 3.8 shows that integrated neighborhoods are more similar to white communities than to
predominantly nonwhite areas. A notable portion of integrated neighborhoods have below-average disadvantage, as is common for white
areas. Yet the conditions of integrated neighborhoods are affected by the
presence of nonwhites; nearly half have above-average disadvantage
compared to only about 11 percent of white areas.

On the whole, racial and ethnic groups reside in qualitatively distinct
social worlds in the United States. Therefore, any description of the
social and economic character of neighborhoods that ignores the role of
race and ethnicity is highly distorted. Indeed, it is quite misleading to
describe neighborhoods in terms of "average" disadvantage because the
vast majority of areas do not have values near 0. Rather, neighborhoods

Table 3.2   Number of Extreme Disadvantages for Neighborhoods of Different Colors

Neighborhood Color	None	Only One	Two or Three	Four or More
White areas	88.9%	4.6%	5.5%	1.0%
African American areas	2.8	12.3	28.6	56.4
Latino areas	3.2	3.8	41.5	51.4
Minority areas	5.9	15.0	31.5	47.6
Integrated areas	56.4	16.5	18.4	8.7

Source: National Neighborhood Crime Study (Peterson and Krivo 2010).

commonly are either white and possess few disadvantages or nonwhite (African American, Latino, or minority) and possess many disadvantages. "Average" levels of deprivation are found mainly in integrated areas. This type of neighborhood is by no means rare (about one-third of the sample); nevertheless, it is far from the norm.

We also compare the *number* of disadvantages that are extremely high across the five ethno-racial community types (table 3.2). At one end of the spectrum, most white areas (89 percent) do not have extreme levels for a single disadvantage characteristic. Integrated neighborhoods are also well off in this regard: 56 percent have no extremely high disadvantages. Only about 3 percent of African American and Latino communities and 6 percent of minority areas are privileged enough that they have no extreme disadvantages. At the other end of the spectrum, we reveal a common pattern of *hyperdisadvantage*—at least four of the six aspects of disadvantage are extreme—among predominantly nonwhite urban neighborhoods. This is the case for over half of African American and Latino neighborhoods and 48 percent of minority communities. In addition to hyperdisadvantaged communities, 29 percent of African American areas, 42 percent of Latino areas, and 32 percent of minority areas have two or three disadvantages that are extremely high. Thus, a full 85 percent of all African American areas are extremely disadvantaged in at least two ways, as are 93 percent of Latino communities, and this is the case as well for nearly 80 percent of minority neighborhoods. Such entrenched disadvantage is rare among white and integrated communities. Virtually no white and very few integrated communities are hyperdisadvantaged. In fact, a mere thirty-one of the over three thousand white neighborhoods in our sample are extremely disadvantaged in four or more ways. And only 7 percent of white and 27 percent of integrated local areas are either hyperdisadvantaged or nearly so, having at least two characteristics at the extreme. Clearly, it is no exaggeration to conclude that minorities and whites live in divergent social worlds.

Other Aspects of Community Character

In addition to disadvantage, urban crime scholars emphasize the roles of residential instability, external investments, and immigrant concentration in accounting for variation in neighborhood crime. How do neighborhoods of color differ across these three characteristics? Table 3.3 addresses this question. Recall that residential instability combines the prevalence of renters and short-term residents. The level of external investment is indicated by the value of home loans. Immigration includes the size of the foreign-born, recent immigrant, and linguistically isolated populations.

As a whole, there is far less ethno-racial differentiation in aspects of residential instability than in either residential loans or immigration. White neighborhoods have many fewer renters than all other types of areas—36 percent for white areas versus 54 to 60 percent for other community types. These gaps reflect long-standing discriminatory housing market practices that limit homeownership for nonwhites, especially for blacks (see, for example, Pager and Shepherd 2008; Ross and Turner 2005). African American neighborhoods have relatively fewer recent movers (41 percent, which is 8 to 15 percent less than in other types of areas). This too is likely due to housing discrimination as well as urban decline. With nonblacks avoiding—or being steered away from—heavily African American neighborhoods, residential mobility into African American areas is low (see, for example, Quillian 2002). Further, many urban African Americans have few options for leaving troubled inner-city neighborhoods. In this sense, they are "stuck" in heavily African American communities. This is not the case for the vast majority of whites, who have more neighborhood options and more resources to facilitate moves (see, for example, Charles 2003; South, Crowder, and Pais 2008). For the other neighborhood types, the presence of recent movers is closer to levels in white areas because of the inflow of new immigrants. Greater mobility within Latino, minority, and integrated areas combines with higher percentages of renters, yielding overall above-average residential instability (0.18 in Latino neighborhoods to 0.28 in integrated areas).

Community investments in the form of residential loans are highly inequitable across communities of distinct colors. While the typical white area received over $22 million in residential loans in 2000, the average African American neighborhood got less than one-quarter of this amount (just under $5 million). Latino and minority neighborhoods are also relatively investment-poor, with an average of $6.5 million and $9.3 million in loans, respectively. Integrated areas are better off than all of the

Table 3.3   Mean Values of Residential Instability and Immigrant Characteristics for Neighborhoods of Different Colors

Neighborhood Characteristic	White Areas	African American Areas	Latino Areas	Minority Areas	Integrated Areas
Residential instability	-.248	-.228	.181	.201	.282
Percentage renters	36.1	55.2	60.8	59.8	54.4
Percentage movers	51.6	41.4	49.8	50.9	56.3
Residential loans (in thousands of dollars)	22,073	4,919	6,485	9,340	14,003
Immigrant characteristics	-.464	-.720	1.934	.630	.259
Percentage foreign-born	8.8	2.8	47.9	26.9	21.3
Percentage recent immigrant	3.7	1.3	21.5	12.5	10.2
Percentage linguistically isolated	2.4	1.3	31.6	14.7	9.4

Source: National Neighborhood Crime Study (Peterson and Krivo 2010).

predominantly nonwhite areas in the amount of residential loans (a mean of $14 million), but lag well behind white neighborhoods.

Racially and ethnically distinct communities vary in the presence of immigrant characteristics in predictable ways. Foreign-born residents, recent immigrants, and the linguistically isolated are most common in predominantly Latino neighborhoods. At the other end of the spectrum, African American areas have very few residents with immigrant characteristics. White, minority, and integrated neighborhoods fall in between the two extremes, with immigration having a stronger presence in the latter two types of areas, owing to the concentration of Latinos.

Conclusion: Linking Divergent Social Worlds and Criminal Inequality

The data presented in this chapter illustrate clearly the dramatic nature of the racial-spatial divide in the urban United States. At issue in this book is whether and how this divide provides the structural underpinnings for racial and ethnic inequality in levels of crime. In chapter 2, we presented a broad overview of violent and property crime rates across distinct ethno-racial neighborhood types. Comparing the rank order of the crime levels across these areas to the order of levels of local contextual characteristics suggests that the hierarchy of crime is indeed closely related to the hierarchy of local circumstances, at least for violent offenses. Specifically, African American neighborhoods have the highest rates of violent crime and also have by far the most disadvantage, the lowest external investments, and the fewest immigrants of all race-ethnic communities. Latino and minority neighborhoods have lower violent crime rates than African American areas, and they have high—but much less extreme—disadvantage levels compared to African American neighborhoods (see figures 3A.5 and 3A.6). Latino and minority areas also have a large immigrant presence, which serves to reduce violence relative to their African American counterparts (Lee, Martinez, and Rosenfeld 2001; Martinez 2002; Sampson 2008; Vélez 2006). Integrated neighborhoods have less disadvantage and considerably higher levels of residential investment than African American, Latino, and minority areas, but their structural circumstances are less favorable than those for their white counterparts. Criminal violence in integrated areas falls between the rate for the African American and minority areas and the rate for white neighborhoods, as do levels of disadvantage and residential investments. As a last point, white areas unquestionably have both the lowest violence rates and the best neighborhood circumstances. Thus, from the comparisons of averages of violence and neighborhood conditions, it appears that racialized community structures are key sources of neighborhood criminal inequality for this type of crime.

Variation in mean property crime rates across neighborhoods of distinct colors does not correspond in a clear fashion with the pattern of structural differentiation in the conditions that undergird crime. Levels of property crime are highest for African American areas, but they are not much greater than those found for integrated communities, even though these two types are quite dissimilar in their structural conditions. For example, integrated neighborhoods receive over three times the amount of loan dollars as African American communities and have much lower levels of disadvantage. Property offenses are also somewhat more common in white than Latino areas. This would not be expected from the patterning of the theoretical community factors, especially given how much less disadvantage there is in white areas.

While informative, the evidence presented to this point does not account for the ways in which neighborhood conditions are linked with one another, and hence it does not allow for an evaluation of their net associations with violent and property crime. Nor does the evidence take into account the relevant criminogenic characteristics of the cities where our sample neighborhoods are located—for example, citywide residential segregation, level of socioeconomic disadvantage for the urban area, and the macroeconomic character that prevails. In the following chapter, we present results from statistical models of neighborhood violent and property crime that simultaneously consider the roles of a full set of relevant neighborhood and city structural characteristics. This approach shows us which factors, at the city and neighborhood levels, are broadly important in predicting local levels of the two types of crime. It also addresses the question of whether racialized neighborhood structures are independently responsible for ethnic and racial neighborhood criminal inequality.

Appendix

Figure 3A.1   Neighborhood Types by Levels of Joblessness

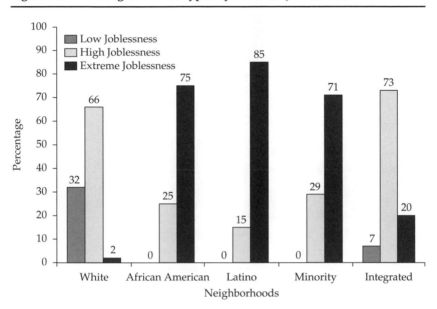

Source: National Neighborhood Crime Study (Peterson and Krivo 2010).

Figure 3A.2   Neighborhood Types with Varying Levels of Low-Wage Jobs

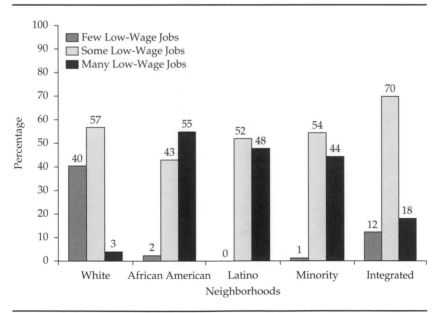

Source: National Neighborhood Crime Study (Peterson and Krivo 2010).

Figure 3A.3   Neighborhood Types with Varying Levels of Female-Headed Families

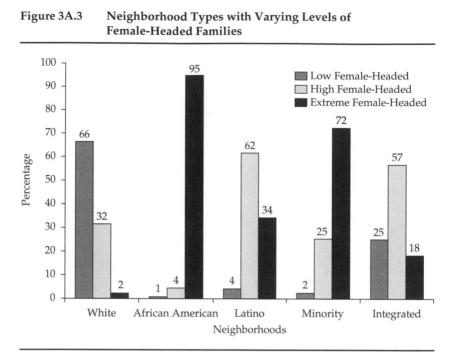

Source: National Neighborhood Crime Study (Peterson and Krivo 2010).

Figure 3A.4   Neighborhood Types with Varying Levels of College Graduates

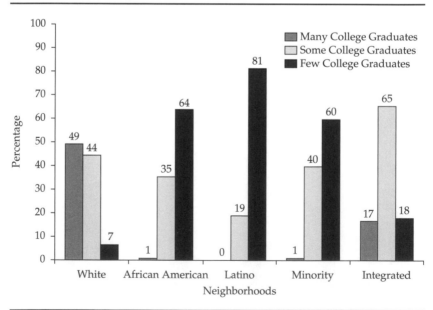

Source: National Neighborhood Crime Study (Peterson and Krivo 2010).

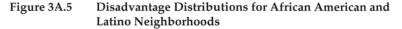

Figure 3A.5   Disadvantage Distributions for African American and Latino Neighborhoods

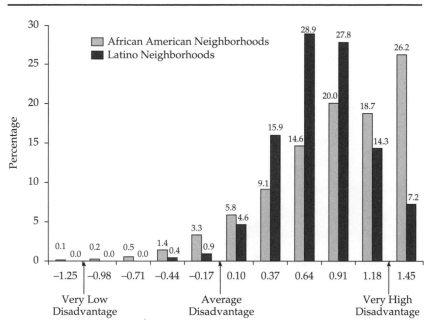

Source: National Neighborhood Crime Study (Peterson and Krivo 2010).
Note: Disadvantage Index values represent the midpoint of equal-size categories.

Figure 3A.6 Disadvantage Distributions for African American and Minority Neighborhoods

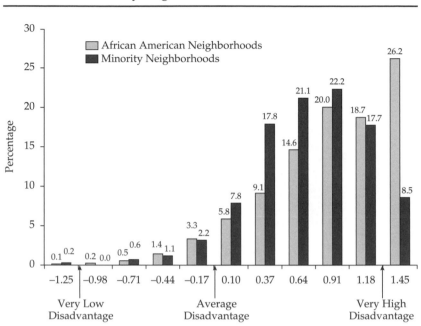

Source: National Neighborhood Crime Study (Peterson and Krivo 2010).
Note: Disadvantage Index values represent the midpoint of equal-size categories.

Chapter 4

The Links Between Racialized Community Structures and Crime

A RE THE divergent social worlds of racially distinct neighborhoods the source of dramatic racial and ethnic neighborhood inequality in violent and property crime? Is crime so low in white neighborhoods because of their enormous socioeconomic privilege? Are the often hyperdisadvantaged conditions of African American local areas responsible for their heightened violent and property offending? Is crime somewhat lower in Latino and minority neighborhoods than in African American ones because the presence of immigrants serves as a countervailing force to high disadvantage? Are integrated areas a middle ground in crime because they fall in the middle in their social and economic character? And do neighborhoods in cities that are more segregated, disadvantaged, and economically declining have worse crime problems?

These important questions have gone unanswered because of the lack of sound national data on neighborhood crime across a diverse set of cities. Here we answer them using the novel National Neighborhood Crime Study, whose breadth of data allows for an unprecedented look at the connections between race, place, and crime. As detailed in this chapter, the extraordinarily divergent social worlds we have already described are at the heart of neighborhood ethno-racial criminal inequality. Yet surprisingly, even after accounting for such divergence, highly *advantaged* nonwhite neighborhoods still have more violence than comparably advantaged white communities.

Structural Conditions and Violent Crime

In chapter 2, we pointed to research showing that city conditions are connected with city rates of violence and that neighborhood conditions and neighborhood violent crime are linked within selected urban areas (see review by Pratt and Cullen 2005). However, we do not know whether and how relationships cross the two levels of city and neighborhood. Therefore, in this section we address two critical questions. Is the character of the city in which neighborhoods are located independently related to neighborhood violence? And are neighborhood structural conditions broadly associated with violent crime across a large set of cities after accounting for variation in city context?

To answer these questions we use multivariate models that examine both neighborhood and city characteristics as predictors of neighborhood violent crime rates. City black-white residential segregation, disadvantage, and manufacturing employment (as an indicator of macroeconomic character) are the key city factors. We also control for city population, region, and the percentages of African Americans, recent movers, foreign-born individuals, and young males. Residential instability, residential loans, immigration, and disadvantage are the core neighborhood conditions we consider, along with the type of race-ethnic neighborhood composition. Neighborhood age structure is controlled. The models account for the fact that different neighborhoods within a given city share commonalities that are not fully captured by measured variables. They also rely on a specification that deals with the relatively rare nature of crime as an outcome.[1] Variables are scaled so that coefficients for the city-level factors (such as segregation) can be interpreted as effects on the average neighborhood violence rate within the city, net of the neighborhood conditions.[2]

Table 4.1 presents results from a model of neighborhood violent crime that includes both the city and neighborhood characteristics. Ethno-racial neighborhood type is included in the model, but the results for this factor are not presented in table 4.1. Findings for racial and ethnic community composition receive major attention in later tables. Each value in table 4.1 represents the percentage change in the rate of neighborhood violent crime for a one-standard-deviation unit change in the respective characteristic.[3] A standard deviation change represents a meaningful but not overwhelming shift in a variable. For example, a difference of one standard deviation in the percentage of African Americans in the city equals 17 percent. This is a large difference in the relative size of the African American population, but one that is clearly observed across cities in the United States. Indeed, it reflects the gap in the size of this population between places such as Denver and Los Angeles, which are about 10 percent African American, and Pittsburgh and Nashville, which are around 27 percent African American. A starred percentage indicates that a condition has a statistically important relationship—that is, one that is clearly different from 0 and is not due to chance.[4]

Are characteristics of cities independently related to neighborhood violence? Residential segregation and manufacturing employment are

Table 4.1   Effects of City and Neighborhood Characteristics on Neighborhood Violent Crime Rates

Characteristic	Percentage Change in Neighborhood Violence
City conditions	
Segregation	28.9%*
Disadvantage	3.7
Percentage manufacturing	−12.5*
Population size	6.9*
Percentage African American	30.2*
Percentage movers	0.5
Percentage foreign-born	7.1
Percentage young males	1.4
South	−21.7*
West	12.2
Neighborhood conditions	
Percentage young males	2.0
Residential instability	29.8*
Residential loans	−8.8*
Immigration	−11.2*
Disadvantage (at the mean)	58.9*

Source: National Neighborhood Crime Study (Peterson and Krivo 2010).
Note: Values represent the percentage change in the neighborhood violent crime rate for a one-standard-deviation unit change in the characteristic for all variables except South and West. For the region variables, values represent the percentage difference in the neighborhood violent crime rate between the South or West and other areas of the country. Ethno-racial neighborhood type is controlled.
*$p < .05$

both important contributors to violence in local areas. Neighborhoods located in cities where black-white segregation is greater have notably higher levels of violent crime. Thus, segregation of urban environments adds to violence over and above the ways in which it concentrates deleterious conditions in African American and other nonwhite neighborhoods and advantageous circumstances in white areas. Specifically, a one-standard-deviation-higher level of segregation (18 points on a 100-point scale) is associated with a nearly 30 percent higher rate of neighborhood-level violence. Thus, the typical neighborhood in a place such as Kansas City, Missouri, or Dallas (segregation value = 66) would have 30 percent more violence than the same neighborhood in a city like New Haven (segregation value = 48). This connection is sizable and suggests that racial residential segregation is indeed harmful to the creation of safe communities. As we argued earlier, city segregation undermines the ability of communities to come together to solve problems. When the public is racially and spatially divided, groups do not have common local interests, and hence the motivation and coalitions required to improve the social and institutional structures that affect crime are likely to be absent.

The macroeconomic character of the larger urban area is also related to neighborhood violence. In particular, a stronger manufacturing base in a city is associated with lower violence for neighborhoods. A one-standard-deviation-higher percentage of workers (a difference of five percentage points) in this type of industry is related to a 12.5 percent lower rate of neighborhood violent crime. Cities with a viable manufacturing economy have many good jobs for residents and a strong tax base for local governments. This means that individuals and institutions have more resources to invest in local communities and hence to support the conventional opportunities for residents that encourage people to stay out of trouble. Manufacturing cities are also more capable of maintaining services such as police, recreation centers, and other functions that help keep crime at bay. The level of citywide socioeconomic disadvantage has only a slight association with neighborhood violence, and one that is not statistically significant net of other city and neighborhood factors. Apparently, city disadvantage and violent crime are linked exclusively through the way in which disadvantage is distributed across neighborhoods.

Beyond the key factors, neighborhood violence is greater in larger cities and in those with more sizable African American populations. The relationship between population size and violence is well established in studies of cities. In contrast, it is surprising that the percentage of African Americans in the urban area is connected with violence when segregation, city disadvantage, and a host of other structural conditions within urban places, as well as disadvantage and racial composition at the neighborhood level, are taken into account. This result may itself reflect aspects of the racialized nature of social and political processes within U.S. cities that are difficult to measure across a broad set of places. For example, many cities with large black populations, such as Detroit and Cleveland, are plagued with substantial financial and institutional problems stemming from long periods of disinvestment and political neglect. This all-encompassing decline has made it extremely difficult to overcome spirals of decay that encourage the spread of problematic outcomes like crime.

The remaining city condition associated with neighborhood violence is location in the South. Neighborhoods in southern cities have nearly 22 percent *less* violent crime than their counterparts elsewhere. Lower violence in southern neighborhoods is unexpected in light of previous theory and research suggesting that there is a southern culture of violence that condones violent behavior as a way of addressing grievances under particular circumstances (see, for example, Nelsen, Corzine, and Huff-Corzine 1994; Parker and Pruitt 2000; Wolfgang and Ferracuti 1967). The unanticipated result reflects the particular cities included in the NNCS. Our sample is representative of large cities overall and within regions. Yet given the size of our city sample, states with very few places over 100,000 population, including large parts of the South, are sometimes not represented in our data. In fact, there are no cities in the sample from the several Deep South states. This may explain the regional effect observed here.

The results presented in the bottom portion of table 4.1 explore whether the associations of neighborhood characteristics with violence found in single-city studies hold in a national sample. In fact, all four of the theoretical structural conditions are statistically connected with rates of violent crime, and they have moderate to very strong influences. Violence within neighborhoods is higher in more residentially unstable and highly disadvantaged areas, while it is lower in places that receive more residential investments and have more immigrants. In particular, a one-standard-deviation-greater level of residential instability is associated with a 30 percent higher level of violent crime. This finding is consistent with social disorganization theory, which contends that more unstable communities have more difficulty coming together to achieve common goals, including crime reduction. More residential loans reduce rates of violence across a large sample of neighborhoods throughout the United States. A notable increase in the amount of loan dollars (one standard deviation) is connected with a nearly 9 percent lower rate of criminal violence. This finding underscores the importance of local investments for shoring up neighborhoods in ways that keep criminal violence at bay. Neighborhoods with a standard-deviation-higher level of immigration have about 11 percent less violence. This finding supports a growing number of recent studies that highlight the beneficial impact of immigrant presence for keeping crime down.

As noted in chapter 2, disadvantage is one of the strongest and most consistent predictors of neighborhood violence (see, for example, Peterson and Krivo 2005; Pratt and Cullen 2005). The results presented here for a national sample of local areas provide further support for this conclusion. However, the influence of disadvantage on violence may taper off as disadvantage becomes increasingly widespread (Krivo and Peterson 2000; McNulty 2001) because once disadvantage becomes very high, ever greater levels may not further differentiate communities in ways that are influential for crime. To illustrate using poverty (one component of disadvantage), consider a 10 percent difference in the poverty rate when going from a low of 10 percent poor to 20 percent poor, compared to a shift from a very high 40 percent poor to 50 percent poor. The former change is likely to have a strong impact on community social organization, and hence violent crime. By contrast, the neighborhood with the very high 40 percent rate is probably already so steeped in disorganization that the same poverty increase would matter little for crime. The NNCS data support this argument. Greater neighborhood disadvantage is associated with more violence, but this effect is weaker for higher compared to lower disadvantage. As shown in table 4.1, when disadvantage is at the average level, one-standard-deviation-more disadvantage is associated with a nearly 60 percent higher rate of violent crime. When disadvantage is very low (one standard deviation below the mean), the same increase results in a 90 percent higher rate of violence (results not reported in table 4.1). And when disadvantage is a similar amount *above* average, a one-standard-deviation increase in this factor leads to just 33 percent more violence. Thus, although the linkage between disadvantage and violence is substantial at all levels, higher and higher deprivation is connected with less and less change in criminal violence.

Accounting for Ethno-Racial Inequality in Neighborhood Violence

The core argument of this book is that racialized neighborhood structures are critical in producing ethnic and racial inequality in neighborhood crime. We contend that racial and ethnic residential segregation is a key structural mechanism that helps to sustain an overall racial hierarchy in the United States. In this segregated context, dramatic inequalities in social conditions are produced and persist across urban neighborhoods that differ in their ethno-racial composition. The variation in circumstances is fundamental in setting the stage for crime and therefore should account for ethno-racial inequality in neighborhood violence.

In this section, we evaluate this argument by exploring differentials in violence across white, African American, Latino, minority, and integrated neighborhoods using the same type of multivariate analysis as reported in table 4.1. Table 4.2 presents these results. The values in this table represent the ratios of the neighborhood violent crime rate for the average African American, Latino, minority, or integrated area to that for the average white area. Our baseline model (row 1) considers ethno-racial differences in violence while simultaneously holding constant city conditions and local-area age-sex composition, but no other neighborhood characteristics. We then add in succession each of the neighborhood factors that is considered to be a major contributor to local violence (rows 2 to 5). Residential instability is considered first, followed by residential loans, immigration, and disadvantage in turn. To the degree that

Table 4.2   Ratios of Violent Crime Rates for African American, Latino, Minority, and Integrated Versus White Neighborhoods

Accounting For:	African American Area/ White Area	Latino Area/ White Area	Minority Area/ White Area	Integrated Area/ White Area
Baseline model	4.27*	2.49*	3.45*	2.25*
Plus residential instability	3.82*	2.46*	3.12*	2.02*
Plus residential loans	3.28*	2.13*	2.80*	1.92*
Plus immigration	3.26*	2.25*	2.87*	1.95*
Plus disadvantage	1.65*	1.29*	1.53*	1.36*

Source: National Neighborhood Crime Study (Peterson and Krivo 2010).
Note: The baseline model includes ten city characteristics (segregation, disadvantage, manufacturing, population, percentage African American, percentage recent movers, percentage foreign-born, percentage young males, South, and West) and neighborhood age-sex structure. Shading highlights the substantial degree of change in the violence ratios from the baseline model to the final model that includes neighborhood disadvantage.
*$p < .05$

racialized social conditions contribute to ethnic and racial inequality in violent crime, the reported violence ratios should fall closer to 1 as each additional neighborhood factor is taken into consideration.

Beginning with the baseline model, differentials in violent crime rates are striking when aspects of the city context and the percentage of young males in the neighborhood are controlled. For the average city, violent crime in African American neighborhoods is just over four and a quarter times that for white neighborhoods (row 1). This very large gap is only slightly less than the differential in mean rates without any factors controlled, where the violent crime rate for African American areas is five times that for white areas (reported in figure 2.1). For the other three neighborhood colors, the excess of average violence compared to whites is also large and barely altered from that for the gross means reported in figure 2.1. Violent crime in Latino areas is about two and a half times higher than in the average white neighborhood. The ratio is similar for integrated areas, where mean violence is about two and a quarter times that for white areas. Minority areas have three and a half times as much violence as typical white neighborhoods.

How much does each neighborhood condition account for these differentials in violent crime? We answer this question first for residential instability (row 2). Although this factor has a strong relationship with neighborhood rates of violent crime (see table 4.1), residential instability accounts for only a small share of differences from white area violence for each distinct neighborhood color. When this community condition is added, the excess of violent crime in African American, minority, and integrated neighborhoods compared to white neighborhoods is reduced by only a modest amount—about 10 percent in each case. For African American areas, the gap is still very large, but the mean falls below four times that for white areas. For minority and integrated neighborhoods, the ratios now drop to slightly more than 3 and 2, respectively, after controlling for differences in residential instability. Finally, the Latino-white gap in neighborhood violence is unaffected by variation in levels of instability.

Next we incorporate external investments, as reflected in greater amounts of residential loan dollars. For each type of neighborhood, residential loans reduce the violence differentials further (comparing rows 2 and 3), with change being more substantial for African American and Latino areas than for either of the other two types of areas. For African American and Latino neighborhoods, the differentials from white communities are reduced by about 15 percent. Thus, the substantial deficits in the infusion of resources into these two types of nonwhite neighborhoods (reported in table 3.3) is a modest, but not unimportant, part of the story underlying violence gaps. This is somewhat less the case for minority and integrated areas. Variation in investments reduces the gap in violence between minority and white neighborhoods by 10 percent and produces a reduction of only 5 percent for integrated areas.

Turning to neighborhood immigration, Latino areas are the most distinguished from other types of communities in the prevalence of immigrant characteristics (table 3.3). Thus, immigration should be a major factor accounting for violent crime in Latino compared to white (and other) neighborhoods. Bear in mind, however, that immigration operates to reduce violence and hence is one condition that keeps Latino rates down and closer to those in white areas. When immigration is held constant in the model, its levels are treated as if they are lower than actually observed in Latino neighborhoods. This would raise violence and increase the difference from white communities. We observe this pattern in table 4.2 with the Latino-white neighborhood violence ratio increasing when immigration is controlled. Thus, it appears that violent crime would be even higher for Latino relative to white neighborhoods if immigration did not work to keep violence down. The addition of immigration to the model is inconsequential in accounting for inequality in violence between African American, minority, and integrated areas compared to white areas because immigration is less common in all of these neighborhood types.

Finally, the results make it clear that socioeconomic disadvantage is the major condition accounting for the much higher levels of violence in all types of nonwhite versus white neighborhoods. Incorporating disadvantage reduces the African American–white ratio by about half. Rates of violence are, on average, 65 percent higher in African American than white neighborhoods after accounting for the large difference in disadvantage between the two types of communities. The remaining differential is still substantial, but it is far short of what is otherwise observed—African American rates that are three to more than four times those for white areas. The incorporation of disadvantage leads to similarly large reductions in the Latino-white and minority-white ratios. These differentials are diminished by 43 and 47 percent, respectively, compared to the model without disadvantage. Disadvantage has a smaller but still strong impact on the integrated versus white violence differential. When all characteristics are accounted for, violent crime is an average of about one-third higher for integrated than white neighborhoods.

Clearly racialized neighborhood structural factors go a long way in accounting for inequality in levels of violent crime across areas with distinct ethno-racial compositions. If dramatic differences in social circumstances by race did not exist in the United States, African American neighborhoods would have average rates of violence only 65 percent higher than for white neighborhoods, not 327 percent higher ($[4.27 - 1.00] \times 100$). Latino, minority, and integrated neighborhoods would have average rates just 29, 53, and 36 percent higher, respectively, than for white areas, not more than two or three times as high (as shown in row 1). Thus, even with such large reductions, racial privilege in violent crime rates for white communities remains and is consequential in magnitude.

The Further Importance of Racialized Disadvantage

Thus far we have demonstrated the centrality of disadvantage as a structural condition underlying criminal violence. Earlier work suggests, however, that the relationship between disadvantage and violence varies across race-ethnic groups and areas because of the differential positions of groups in society. Along with Thomas McNulty, we have shown that disadvantage is more strongly connected with white than African American rates of violence (Krivo and Peterson 2000; McNulty 2001). This results from whites living in the privileged situation of low disadvantage. Increases in this condition are meaningful in distinguishing criminogenic structural contexts, but this is not the case for African Americans, who commonly live in areas where disadvantage is very high and changes in levels do not produce strong qualitative distinctions in structural environments. In other words, predominantly white and African American areas are in non-overlapping parts of the disadvantage distribution where the influences of deprivation are dissimilar.

The results for disadvantage reported so far for the NNCS data appear to be consistent with these earlier findings. Broadly speaking, we have shown that disadvantage: (1) differentiates neighborhoods of distinct colors such that not all types of areas are found throughout the disadvantage distribution; and (2) has a relationship with violence that changes across its own levels. Combining these two facts leads us to expect different effects of disadvantage on violence across the differentially situated ethno-racial neighborhoods, with the relationship being strongest for white areas and weakest for African American locales. Here we will assess this hypothesis and elucidate how the results increase our understanding of the structural dynamics that lead to inequality in neighborhood violent crime.

To do so, we modified the model of violent crime (from the last row of table 4.2) to allow the impact of disadvantage to vary across the five types of neighborhoods of color (coefficients not reported, but see figure 4.1).[5] The relationship of disadvantage with violence indeed differs across the types of areas. As expected, this linkage is most substantial for white neighborhoods, consistently the weakest for African American areas, and in between for the other types of communities. Further, in African American, Latino, and integrated neighborhoods, the influ-

Figure 4.1   Predicted Violent Crime Rates for Observed Levels of Disadvantage for Ethno-Racial Neighborhood Types

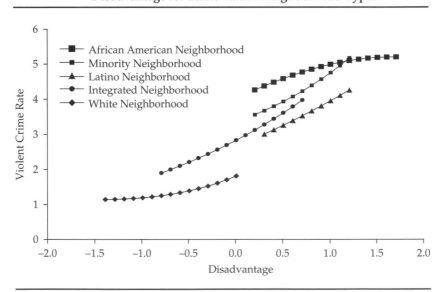

Source: National Neighborhood Crime Study (Peterson and Krivo 2010).

ence of disadvantage on criminal violence tapers off at higher disadvantage levels.

The diminishing connection between disadvantage and violence is particularly pronounced for African American neighborhoods. In fact, when disadvantage is at or above the very high mean level that exists for this population, its association with violent crime rates is very small. As we argued, variation at the very high levels widely found in African American neighborhoods does not alter the social organization of communities in ways that are influential for violent crime. Of course, Latino and minority neighborhoods also suffer from concentrations of disadvantaged characteristics and thus should experience a similar drop-off in the association of disadvantage with violence. We find this pattern to a modest degree for Latino areas but not for minority areas. Neither of these community types has the stark prevalence of extreme disadvantage found in African American urban neighborhoods, which is why the leveling off may not be pronounced. Over one-quarter of African American areas in our sample have the most extreme disadvantage. Thus, they are unique even when compared to Latino and minority neighborhoods, where only 7.2 and 8.5 percent, respectively, are extremely disadvantaged (figures 3.6 and 3.7).

How do the differential relationships combine with variation in disadvantage levels across ethno-racial neighborhood types in producing inequality in violent crime? To answer this question, figure 4.1 provides a dramatic depiction of violent crime rates by neighborhood color and disadvantage. This figure presents predicted rates of violent crime (per 1,000 population) for neighborhoods between the tenth and ninetieth percentiles of observed disadvantage separately for each neighborhood color. Thus, the figure displays net rates of violent crime within the ranges of neighborhood disadvantage widely found for each group in urban areas in the United States.

The patterns highlight that ethno-racial groups live in divergent social worlds, with clear and dramatic implications for inequality in neighborhood violent crime. Predicted violence rates for observed white areas are exclusively in the left half of the graph, where disadvantage is low, while predicted rates for observed African American, Latino, and minority areas are entirely in the right half of the figure, where disadvantage ranges from above average to extreme. Thus, even the *most* disadvantaged white neighborhoods have an average violent crime rate of 1.8 per 1,000, which is much lower than rates in the *least* disadvantaged areas of any of the three types of nonwhite neighborhoods. The range is from 3.0 in Latino to 4.3 in African American neighborhoods. When the positive effect of disadvantage combines with very high levels, violent crime reaches peak rates of 4.3 in Latino and 5.2 in minority neighborhoods. The violence rate is consistently higher in African American areas than in all other types of areas, reaching a maximum of 5.2 per 1,000 in the large proportion of neighborhoods that have extreme levels of disadvantage. This is the case despite the fact that the influence of this factor levels off among African American neighborhoods that are extremely disadvantaged.

Predicted rates of violence for integrated areas fall squarely between those for white areas and those for the other three groups. Integrated communities tend to have levels of disadvantage that range from low to moderate. This is also generally true for levels of violence, which are just under 2 at the low end of observed disadvantage but rise to approximately 4 when disadvantage is near its highest level. Finally, and compared to other areas, white neighborhoods are decidedly privileged in the low levels of violent crime that emanate from their extremely low levels of disadvantage. Predicted rates are just above 1 per 1,000 for a large portion of white neighborhoods. Although violence is higher in more disadvantaged white areas, rates never reach levels as high as those found for other types of neighborhoods.

Some of the inequality in violence is not accounted for by where racially and ethnically distinct neighborhoods are situated in their levels of disadvantage, or by the differential effects of disadvantage. Figure 4.1 shows this in notable jumps in predicted rates between white communities and each of the other four areas. Thus, it appears that white areas garner privileges that enable them to create neighborhoods that are dramatically safer than those of other groups. In contrast, much of the differentiation in violence among the other ethno-racial areas appears to be the product of how the racial structure of society places groups in divergent social worlds. This is suggested by the rather continuous picture of rates for integrated neighborhoods and the three predominantly non-white neighborhoods. Predicted rates for integrated areas flow directly down from those for the other types of communities. By implication, rates for these areas would be markedly similar if they had more comparable levels of disadvantage. As such, ethnic and racial inequality in neighborhood violence is maintained through broadly racialized forces that keep groups separate and unequal and whites more privileged than others.

Structural Conditions and Property Crime

How do the patterns of findings for property crime compare to those for violence? Property crime is much more common than violent crime, but varies considerably across neighborhoods. Thus, as with violence, we ask: Are levels of property crime responsive to the character of the city where neighborhoods are located? And are neighborhood structural conditions broadly associated with property offense rates after

Table 4.3   Effects of City and Neighborhood Characteristics on Neighborhood Property Crime Rates

Characteristic	Percentage Change in Neighborhood Property Crime
City conditions	
Segregation	4.1%
Disadvantage	6.6
Percentage manufacturing	−5.8
City population	4.7
Percentage African American	1.3
Percentage movers	2.2
Percentage foreign-born	−1.5
Percentage young males	1.0
South	−7.5
West	−6.0
Neighborhood conditions	
Percentage young males	1.0
Residential instability	27.2*
Residential loans	−9.4*
Immigration	−14.7*
Disadvantage (at the mean)	15.2*

Source: National Neighborhood Crime Study (Peterson and Krivo 2010).
Note: Values represent the percentage change in the neighborhood property crime rate for a one-standard-deviation unit change in the characteristic for all variables except South and West. For the region variables, values represent the percentage difference in the neighborhood property crime rate between the South or West and other areas of the country. Ethno-racial neighborhood type is controlled.
*$p < .05$

accounting for variation in city context? In examining these questions, we use the same type of multivariate models we used for neighborhood violence. Table 4.3 presents percentage changes in rates of neighborhood property crime for a one-standard-deviation unit change in each predictor variable.

The first point of note is that none of the city characteristics has a statistically important association with neighborhood property crime. Thus, it appears that these types of offenses are equally prevalent in all types of cities. The second general pattern is that all of the central neighborhood factors are related to property crime rates in the same way as with criminal violence. Offense rates are higher in areas that are more unstable and disadvantaged. Rates are notably lower for neighborhoods that receive greater infusions of loans and have more immigrants. The sizes of these relationships are similar to those for violent crime for three of the four conditions examined. A notably higher (one standard deviation) level of residential instability is associated with a 27 percent higher rate of property offending. Conversely, an equal amount of change in dollars invested in residential loans is associated with over 9 percent less property crime. The trade-off for a one-standard-deviation-greater level of immigration is nearly 15 percent less property crime.

The impact of disadvantage on property offending is not as strong as for violent crime. As before, however, the connection between disadvantage and property crime is stronger when disadvantage is low, and it weakens as levels increase. At mean disadvantage, a 15 percent higher property crime rate would be observed if disadvantage was one standard deviation higher. At a much lower level of disadvantage—one standard deviation below the mean—we would expect a 34 percent higher rate for a similar increase. By the time disadvantage is considerably above the average, the association is essentially zero.

In sum, the results for property crime are largely consistent with those for neighborhood predictors of violence. Neighborhood instability and disadvantage are important structural sources of both types of offending. Further, disadvantage is less strongly connected with property and violent crime when levels of this community condition are very high and there is less substantive differentiation in the social contexts that generate crime. However, disadvantage is more weakly associated with property than violence rates throughout most of the disadvantage distribution. The findings also provide evidence for the relevance of external investments in local areas as significant resources that help neighborhoods maintain viability in ways that keep property crime low, which is also true for violence. Finally, immigration's negative relationship with violent and property crime makes it clear that the presence of immigrants in local communities is highly beneficial for reducing neighborhood crime.

Accounting for Ethno-Racial Inequality in Neighborhood Property Crime

Ethno-racial neighborhood inequality in property crime is not as dramatic as for violence. There are differences in the mean levels for different types of areas, but there is much more overlap in the distributions of property offenses compared with violent offenses. Reported property offending is highest, on average, in African American neighborhoods, but the mean and spread of rates is not much different than for integrated areas. Also, average levels of property crime are similarly low for Latino and white areas. As we noted at the end of chapter 3, the simple

Table 4.4   Ratios of Property Crime Rates for Black, Latino, Minority, and Integrated Versus White Neighborhoods

Accounting For:	African American Area/ White Area	Latino Area/ White Area	Minority Area/ White Area	Integrated Area/ White Area
Baseline model	1.58*	1.03	1.34*	1.30*
Plus residential instability	1.47*	1.04	1.27*	1.21*
Plus residential loans	1.32*	0.94	1.17*	1.17*
Plus immigration	1.28*	1.20*	1.30*	1.25*
Plus disadvantage	1.10	1.08	1.11*	1.08*

Source: National Neighborhood Crime Study (Peterson and Krivo 2010).
Note: The baseline model includes ten city characteristics (segregation, disadvantage, manufacturing, population, percentage African American, percentage recent movers, percentage foreign-born, percentage young males, South, and West) and neighborhood age-sex structure. Shading highlights the substantial degree of change in the violence ratios from the baseline model to the final model that includes neighborhood disadvantage.
*$p < .05$

rank ordering of mean property crime rates across neighborhoods of distinct colors does not correspond well with the ordering of the levels of social conditions thought to underlie crime. Here we assess whether the roles of neighborhood factors in race-ethnic differences in property crime are masked by not simultaneously controlling for local conditions and city characteristics. Table 4.4 reports these findings from the same type of multivariate model presented in previous tables. As with violent crime, values represent the ratio of the neighborhood property crime rate for the average African American, Latino, minority, or integrated area to that for the average white area. The relevance of neighborhood conditions in generating ethno-racial inequality in property crime is reflected in the degree to which the ratios fall closer to 1 as each neighborhood factor is taken into account.

The baseline model shows that property crime rates for neighborhoods in the average city are nearly 60 percent higher for African American than white areas (row 1). The gaps are smaller when comparing minority or integrated neighborhoods to those where whites predominate. In both cases, property crime is about one-third higher than for their white counterparts. In contrast, Latino areas do not differ substantially from white neighborhoods. The net similarity in property crime rates for these two types of areas mirrors that found for the gross rates in figure 2.1. After adding residential instability (row 2), gaps in rates relative to white communities are reduced somewhat for all types of areas except where Latinos predominate; in those areas, comparable levels still hold. Residential loans are associated with about a 10 percent reduction in property crime differentials for African American and minority neighborhoods compared to white neighborhoods (compare rows 2 and 3). Nonetheless, rates are 32 percent higher for African American areas, and 17 percent higher for minority areas, than for white areas. Increased investments through residential loans are important in keeping property crime down (as seen in table 4.3), but they do little to account for higher property crime in integrated neighborhoods compared to white ones.

Next, we add immigration. Property crime rates would be slightly closer for African American and white communities if immigration levels were similar. However, for the other three comparisons, differentials in average property crime would be greater than otherwise observed if immigration was comparable. Indeed, Latino areas would have 20 percent more property offenses than white neighborhoods if immigration was equalized. Before taking this factor into account, rates were statistically similar in these two types of areas. Accounting for immigration, minority areas have 30 percent more property crime, and integrated areas 25 percent more than white neighborhoods. These results stem from the direction of the impact of the presence of immigrants on property crime and the varying levels of immigration found across types of areas. Immigrant concentration is very high in Latino neighborhoods and modest to high in integrated and minority areas. Thus, controlling for immigration implies a lower level of immigrant concentration in these three types of communities than is typical for them. Because immigration suppresses property crime, one would observe higher levels of such crime in Latino, minority, and integrated areas, overall and relative to white areas, if there were fewer immigrants in the communities.

The final row of table 4.4 reports property crime gaps after controlling for neighborhood socioeconomic disadvantage. Property crime in African American and Latino areas is statistically indistinguishable from rates in white neighborhoods when this important condition is taken into account. Rates are only about 10 percent higher for minority areas, and 8 percent higher for integrated areas, than for comparable white neighborhoods when disadvantage is held constant. While statistically different from 0, these gaps are substantively small. In sum, local structural conditions appear to be most of the reason for differences in property crime across communities of distinct colors. This contrasts with the picture for violence, where differences in neighborhood characteristics do *not* fully account for the gaps in observed rates, even though these factors are responsible for much of the inequality in violent offending across ethno-racial neighborhood types.

Inequality in Crime in Advantaged Neighborhoods

The data presented to this point underscore the importance of racialized local conditions as structural forces that generate neighborhood ethno-racial inequality in crime. However, why do neighborhood structural differentials not completely account for the crime gaps, particularly with regard to violence? A possible answer lies in the very nature of the inter-connections between race, socioeconomic position, and other structural conditions that lead to the relative absence of racially and ethnically distinct but economically comparable neighborhoods. We attempted to address this challenge by collecting NNCS data, which include a large sample of neighborhoods across the United States. Yet as the descriptive data presented in chapter 3 show so clearly, the racial-spatial divide that permeates U.S. society is so great that our results may still be partially tainted by the lack of comparability of social conditions across distinct neighborhoods of color. That is, to some extent the analyses reported to this point may still be comparing the combined privileges of white race and middle- or upper-class status in white neighborhoods with the bur-dens of subordinate race-ethnicity and socioeconomic status that pervade in other localities.

Here we take an additional step to address the fundamental struc-tural comparability problem for research. Specifically, we analyze sets of local areas that are all relatively *advantaged* to assess whether non-white communities have equally low levels of crime when they are appar-ently as well off as their white counterparts. Put differently, are levels of violent and property crime more similar when the association between race and economic composition is less dramatic? Only two previous studies of individual cities hint at the answer to this question. Our own investigation of reported rates of violent crime in 1990 for cen-sus tracts in Columbus, Ohio (Krivo and Peterson 1996) focused on this city because it is a fruitful site for studying racially distinct but econom-ically similar neighborhoods: it has some white high-poverty areas as well as some African American economically advantaged areas. We demonstrated that African American and white neighborhoods with similarly low, high, or extreme levels of disadvantage have compara-ble levels of violent and property crime. McNulty (2001) studied neigh-borhoods in Atlanta for 1990. He also compared rates of violence between white and black areas because there were enough African American neighborhoods with below-average disadvantage to make comparisons between racially distinct and economically similar areas. His analysis demonstrated that violent crime rates are quite similar when neighbor-hoods have comparably low disadvantage.

Table 4.5   Ratios of Violent Crime Rates for African American, Latino, Minority, and Integrated Versus White Low-Poverty Neighborhoods

Accounting For:	African American Area/ White Area	Latino Area/ White Area	Minority Area/ White Area	Integrated Area/ White Area
Baseline model	3.26*	1.71*	2.55*	1.76*
Plus residential instability	3.40*	1.90*	2.61*	1.71*
Plus residential loans	3.17*	1.76*	2.45*	1.65*
Plus immigration	3.12*	1.89*	2.54*	1.69*
Plus disadvantage	2.12*	1.39*	1.70*	1.34*

Source: National Neighborhood Crime Study (Peterson and Krivo 2010).
Note: The baseline model includes ten city characteristics (segregation, disadvantage, manufacturing, population, percentage African American, percentage recent movers, percentage foreign-born, percentage young males, South, and West) and neighborhood age-sex structure. Low poverty is defined as less than 20 percent poor. Shading highlights the substantial degree of change in the violence ratios from the baseline model to the final model that includes neighborhood disadvantage.
$*p < .05$

The NNCS data allow us to examine the validity of the conclusions from these two cities for a large number of U.S. neighborhoods that are white, African American, Latino, minority, or integrated and comparatively advantaged. Specifically, we focus on the subset of neighborhoods with *low* rates of poverty (less than 20 percent).[6] Of the 5,495 low-poverty areas in the 87 cities studied here, 326 are African American, 149 are Latino, and 171 are minority. These low-poverty nonwhite areas include between one-fifth and one-quarter of each type of predominantly nonwhite area. Reflecting the overall sample and U.S. society, 2,890 of the low-poverty neighborhoods are white and 1,959 are integrated.

Table 4.5 reports the nonwhite-to-white ratios of violent crime among low-poverty neighborhoods. Despite their low poverty, violent crime rates are significantly higher for all predominantly nonwhite communities than for their white counterparts. This is unexpectedly consistent with the picture for the full set of neighborhoods. The baseline gap is greatest when comparing African American to white local areas. Rates are three and a quarter times higher for the former communities than for the latter. Minority low-poverty areas have about two and a half times as much violence as similar white neighborhoods, while Latino and integrated communities have about 70 to 75 percent more criminal violence than white areas. These differentials are substantial, but notably smaller than for the full sample of neighborhoods, where the gaps in violent

Table 4.6   Ratios of Property Crime Rates for African American,
            Latino, Minority, and Integrated Versus
            White Low-Poverty Neighborhoods

Accounting For:	African American Area/ White Area	Latino Area/ White Area	Minority Area/ White Area	Integrated Area/ White Area
Baseline model	1.42*	0.94	1.24*	1.15*
Plus residential instability	1.49*	1.06	1.28*	1.13*
Plus residential loans	1.40*	0.98	1.21*	1.09*
Plus immigration	1.34*	1.19*	1.33*	1.16*
Plus disadvantage	1.17*	1.06	1.10	1.05

Source: National Neighborhood Crime Study (Peterson and Krivo 2010).
Note: The baseline model includes ten city characteristics (segregation, disadvantage, manufacturing, population, percentage African American, percentage recent movers, percentage foreign-born, percentage young males, South, and West) and neighborhood age-sex structure. Low poverty is defined as less than 20 percent poor. Shading highlights the substantial degree of change in the violence ratios from the baseline model to the final model that includes neighborhood disadvantage.
*$p < .05$

crime range from two and a quarter to four and a quarter times those for white areas.

Looking down each column, differences across the distinct ethno-racial communities in residential instability, residential loans, and immigration are not very important in accounting for gaps in violence from white areas. Indeed, when these local conditions are included in the model, differentials in average rates of violent crime are nearly as large—or even larger for the Latino-white comparison—as when only city characteristics and neighborhood age-sex composition are controlled. Differences in disadvantage within these *supposedly comparable* neighborhoods are responsible for a notable portion of the remaining ethno-racial inequality in violence. Yet they by no means account for all of the gaps in violent crime. Even when only low-poverty neighborhoods are examined, African American areas have more than twice the average violent crime rate as their white counterparts. Latino, minority, and integrated neighborhoods have 1.4, 1.7, and 1.3 times as much violence, respectively, as white communities. These net gaps are even larger than those found for the full set of neighborhoods.

Table 4.6 presents the results for property crime among low-poverty neighborhoods. Among advantaged areas, ethnic and racial inequality in property crime is considerably less than for rates of violence. Latino and white neighborhoods have similar levels of property crime, except under the scenario where immigration, but not disadvantage, is controlled. Recall that immigration suppresses crime; therefore, property offenses would rise if Latino communities had the same low presence of immigrants as other types of areas. When we take into account the four structural neighborhood conditions, property crime in low-poverty minority and integrated areas is not distinguishable from that for comparable white areas. African American low-poverty neighborhoods still have statistically higher property crime rates than is the case for white communities (final row), but the differential is just 17 percent (slightly higher than in the full sample of local areas; see table 4.4).

Conclusion: Internal Characteristics and Beyond

In this section, we asked whether there is greater comparability in violent and property crime across neighborhoods of different colors with similarly low levels of poverty. This question is more relevant for violent than property crime because *net* race-ethnic differences in property offending are so small. For violence, the answer is a resounding no. After accounting for the conditions discussed from structural race, urban, and criminological perspectives, race-ethnic gaps in violent crime are as large, or larger, for low-poverty areas as for the full set of neighborhoods. It is not entirely clear why inequalities in crime remain across race-ethnic neighborhoods. However, thinking broadly about the interconnections of race and space in U.S. society, perhaps it is not enough to limit our focus to the influence of the internal conditions of neighborhoods on inequality in crime. Broader spatial processes may also be important. Neighborhoods are situated relative to one another in ways that further differentiate the contexts that may undergird patterns of crime (Mears and Bhati 2006; Morenoff, Sampson, and Raudenbush 2001). In the following chapter, we explore whether the spatial location of neighborhoods of distinct colors helps to provide a more complete answer to the apparently intransigent inequality in crime.

= Chapter 5 =

The Spatial Context of Criminal Inequality

THE BASIC framework presented here emphasizes that ethnic and racial differentials in crime patterns are rooted in the racial inequality embedded in distinct conditions found across and within urban neighborhoods. The evidence is consistent with this framework whether all neighborhoods are studied or analyses are restricted to apparently more comparable low-poverty areas. However, notable gaps in violence remain unaccounted for by racialized community conditions; this is much less the case for property offenses. In this chapter, we acknowledge that the focus on differentiation in structural conditions *within* segregated white, African American, and other nonwhite neighborhoods may be too limited. Such an approach overlooks the embeddedness of neighborhoods within a broader spatial context. In fact, criminogenic neighborhood effects may not end at the borders of local communities (see Mears and Bhati 2006). Neighborhoods are located relative to one another in ways that may reduce or increase crime. And racially and ethnically distinct neighborhoods in U.S. cities are highly unequal in the structural conditions of their surrounding neighborhoods.

In this chapter, we explore how inequality in the character of nearby neighborhoods contributes to patterned racial and ethnic differentials in crime and thereby helps complete the story of the structural underpinnings of such patterns. A common feature of many African American neighborhoods, whatever their internal character, is proximity to communities with characteristics typically associated with higher crime rates, such as high levels of disadvantage and residential turnover. This is also the case, to varying degrees, for Latino and other nonwhite neighborhoods. In contrast, white areas are often surrounded by neighborhoods where crime-promoting conditions are relatively absent and factors that discourage crime, such as external community investments, are prevalent.

We begin by outlining how the structural character of nearby local areas may influence crime rates within focal neighborhoods. We then evaluate whether race-ethnic variation in the concentration of disadvantage, residential instability, immigration, community investments, and white residents in surrounding neighborhoods helps account for ethnoracial inequality in violent and property crimes.

The Role of Nearby Neighborhoods

Neighborhoods are likely to be part of a broader system of linked territories that affect one another. Janet Heitgerd and Robert Bursik (1987, 776) made this point over twenty years ago when they argued that the greatest shortcoming of traditional social disorganization theory lies in "an overriding emphasis on the internal dynamics of local communities that wholly ignore[s] the external contingencies that may be important in shaping the nature of these dynamics. . . . This emphasis [gives] the impression that the local communities of an urban area [are] relatively isolated in a social sense."

An exclusive focus on the internal dynamics of neighborhoods is out of sync with theories of urban structure that conceptualize local communities as having symbiotic relationships that affect processes and outcomes (see, for example, Berry and Kasarda 1977; Hawley 1950, 1981; Heitgerd and Bursik 1987; Morenoff, Sampson, and Raudenbush 2001). In view of this concern, Heitgerd and Bursik (1987) conducted what appears to be the first quantitative investigation of the role of extra-community influences on crime and delinquency. Their finding that delinquency rates in Chicago neighborhoods were affected by conditions in adjacent areas supported the argument that the situation of communities relative to one another is consequential.

Since this publication, technical advances in Geographic Information Systems (GIS) and spatial modeling applications have allowed for increasingly sophisticated tests of whether communities affect one another in ways that influence crime. For example, during the 1990s researchers found that the borders of individual neighborhoods can be quite porous, with violence diffusing from one area to another (see, for example, Cohen and Tita 1999a, 1999b; Messner et al. 1999; Rosenfeld, Bray, and Egley 1999). More recent studies support this conclusion by showing that violence is greater in local areas when there is more violence in neighboring communities (see Browning 2009; Browning, Feinberg, and Dietz 2004; Browning et al. 2010; Hipp 2007; Morenoff, Sampson, and Raudenbush 2001; Rosenfeld, Fornango, and Rengifo 2007; Smith, Frazee, and Davison 2000). However, such research has not evaluated the substantive processes that underlie the spread of criminal violence. Therefore, we do not know if the diffusion stems from common community social processes related to disadvantage, social networks and chains of retaliation, or any other specific social mechanism.

This has become a key concern for neighborhood crime researchers, who are now taking steps to address this issue (Mears and Bhati 2006; Morenoff, Sampson, and Raudenbush 2001; Peterson and Krivo 2009b; Tita and Greenbaum 2009). Along these lines, Jeffrey Morenoff and his colleagues (2001) have demonstrated that lethal violence in Chicago neighborhoods is driven, in part, by *exposure* to heightened disadvantage in areas closer to one's own neighborhood (see also Sampson, Morenoff, and Earls 1999). George Tita and Robert Greenbaum (2009) specifically compare how Pittsburgh neighborhoods with rival gangs affect one another's rates of gang violence to the way bordering neighborhoods influence each other's experience of this type of violence. While rival gang communities have more gang violence, Tita and Greenbaum find that simply being located next to a neighborhood with more gang violence has no such effect.[1] Daniel Mears and Avinash Bhati (2006) assess whether resource deprivation in adjacent neighborhoods or in "socially similar" areas located throughout the city is connected with neighborhood homicide in Chicago. They find that higher levels of resource deprivation in socially similar areas has a strong relationship with lethal violence that also accounts for any apparent impact of deprivation in immediately surrounding areas.[2] These few analyses are highly suggestive of the need to identify how substantive aspects of neighborhoods influence crime across neighborhood boundaries. Yet they beg the question because they explore just two cities, examine the influence across communities of only a single condition, and, except for Mears and Bhati (2006), do not apply direct measures of the important substantive characteristics of other areas. As a consequence, this work leaves unexplored how a range of social conditions in nearby areas produces crime across communities and whether such effects account for differences in levels of offending across neighborhoods of different colors.

We take up the task of exploring how a variety of substantive features of nearby communities affect crime in neighborhoods throughout the United States. Specifically, we ask: to what extent and why do the spatial locations of ethnically and racially distinct neighborhoods yield dissimilar levels of crime? Ethno-racially distinct communities are differentially situated with respect to spatial proximity to areas with higher or lower levels of crime-producing social conditions. Mary Pattillo-McCoy's (1999) study of the middle-class African American neighborhood of "Groveland" highlights the stark contrast in the conditions that surround black compared to white neighborhoods of similar class composition. The average poverty rate in areas surrounding Groveland was 60 percent higher than in Groveland itself; four of the seven neighboring areas had approximately twice Groveland's rate. Pattillo-McCoy contends that this pattern is common among African American neighborhoods but rare for white middle-class areas. Little research has made the types of comparisons needed to broadly confirm this contention. However, a study of two comparably middle-class communities in Columbus, Ohio—one African American and one white—shows a similar pattern for 2000 (Krivo, Peterson, and Karafin 2006). The poverty rate for the African American neighborhood was 4.8 percent, with an average in the areas that surrounded it of 11.8 percent. This compares with 2.6 percent in the white neighborhood, and 5.9 percent in its adjacent communities.

Pattillo-McCoy's (1999) qualitative assessment of Groveland is helpful in explicating how proximity to areas with high levels of social deprivation and other detrimental conditions creates unique risks for crime. Residents of Groveland and of neighboring communities that are more high-risk cross neighborhood boundaries to socialize, shop, attend church, and the like. Adolescents also share schools, particularly high schools, for which catchment areas are larger than a single neighborhood. These types of cross-boundary interactions contribute to crime-producing processes in nearby areas that spill over and directly influence levels of crime in ways that would not be expected from Groveland's middle-class status. For example, Pattillo-McCoy notes that public drug-selling is rare in the community owing to the informal control that, ironically, is exercised by drug kingpins who reside there and want to protect the community from this type of crime. Yet repercussions from the drug trade, such as violent encounters over territory and money, spill over into Groveland.

What are the particular characteristics of neighboring communities that spill over and directly heighten (or reduce) crime within neighborhoods net of these same conditions within the focal area, and through what processes? Our answer draws on Pattillo-McCoy's substantive insights and social disorganization theory. Taken together, these perspectives suggest that neighborhood disadvantage, residential instability, immigration, community investments, and the presence of white residents are the critical factors at play. If areas adjacent to a given neighborhood have high levels of disadvantage (joblessness, poverty, single-parent households, and the like), crime in that neighborhood may be increased as the permeability of borders allows for a broader span of exposure to unconventional role models, situations of company that are conducive to violence, and perceived criminal opportunities. At the same time, effective social control of crime might be undermined from being located in the midst of geographically widespread disadvantage that destabilizes the institutions that offer formal and informal social control and weakens connections to the powerful outside political actors who facilitate public (formal) social control.

Rates of crime could also be increased by having high turnover among nearby community residents because frequent moving hinders the formation of the expansive networks of interpersonal relationships that facilitate informal control. Further, widespread residential instability undermines the local institutions that keep people engaged in conventional activities by providing jobs and services that benefit populations from multiple areas. Being ensconced in a geographic area where outside investments are highly limited might have similar effects on local infrastructures, thereby leading to heightened crime for neighborhoods. Investments are also needed to keep at bay physical deterioration and disorder, which have been linked to crime. Encroachments on order may occur if surrounding areas are unable to garner outside resources. In contrast, location within proximity to areas with substantial outside investments may reflect the presence of powerful political and economic connections that allow communities to fight potential threats that could lead to crime.

A larger presence of immigrants and whites in surrounding neighborhoods might reduce crime in areas beyond what would otherwise be expected when these factors are prevalent only in the focal area. The presence of a sizable immigrant population within a neighborhood is associated with lower rates of crime and violence (see, for example, Lee and Martinez 2002; Sampson 2008). We evaluate whether an additional protective effect is observed when a neighborhood is located within a *broader* immigrant context than when it is treated as an isolated immigrant area.

White neighborhoods are highly privileged in ways that are associated with reduced crime. Although this is partly due to economic advantage, areas clustered among white neighborhoods may have social networks that span larger geographic areas and as such facilitate greater informal social control. White areas may also be linked through political and economic connections that facilitate public social control—that is, they have the capacity to draw resources relevant to crime control from outside sources (Bursik and Grasmick 1993; Vélez 2001). However, benefits may be realized even in the absence of formal ties. In the racialized United States, white racial status often helps generate connections to politically and economically powerful actors when threats to community safety arise (Squires and Kubrin 2006). Larger spans of white areas are also often distant from poverty and other economic sources of crime. In essence, neighborhoods that are ensconced within broader white areas may benefit from an added capacity for social control and from being sealed off from violence and other unsafe activities. As such, these areas may have the character of defended communities (Suttles 1972).

In brief, there are reasons to expect that the spatial patterning of neighborhood conditions underlies variation in crime across neighborhoods of distinct colors. In the following section, we evaluate the extent to which this is the case. The methods we use allow us not only to explore

whether surrounding neighborhoods matter for crime but also to identify which aspects of nearby communities influence crime rates. That is,
our approach allows for a direct assessment of the roles of the specific
substantive factors suggested in Pattillo-McCoy (1999) and earlier analyses of social disorganization.

Spatial Inequality and Crime

How much do the distinct spatial contexts in which white, African
American, Latino, minority, and integrated neighborhoods are located
contribute to varying levels of crime within these communities? To
address this question we add a set of substantive spatial indicators to the
models of violent and property crime described in the previous chapter.
This allows us to evaluate whether the character of neighboring areas
accounts for differentials in crime over and above the differences produced by the internal character of neighborhoods. We include factors
representing levels of disadvantage, residential instability, immigration,
community investments, white residents, and crime in surrounding
neighborhoods. Each spatial variable represents the average level of the
characteristic for neighborhoods that are spatially adjacent to the focal
area.[3] For example, the spatial disadvantage measure for a given neighborhood indicates the average disadvantage across all areas that share
a border with the neighborhood. To illustrate, figure 5.1 presents data
for disadvantage, percentage white, and the violent crime rate for the
three Los Angeles census tracts described at the start of chapter 2 (bold
borders), along with these same data for the areas immediately adjacent
to them. The spatial measures of these three variables (on the far right)
are the averages of the values for the *set* of surrounding neighborhoods.
The white area has very low levels of disadvantage (−1.05) and violent
crime (rate of 5.2) among its neighbors, who are also on average over
80 percent white. Disadvantage and violence are dramatically higher
in the tracts surrounding the African American community; this area
also has almost no whites in the neighborhoods that border it. The spatial circumstances of the Latino area are relatively similar to those for
the African American neighborhood in terms of disadvantage and the
number of white neighbors, but there is noticeably less violence in the
surrounding areas.

   Table 5.1 presents the mean levels of each of the spatial variables for
the five neighborhood types. Neighborhoods that surround white areas
are considerably better off than all other community types in some
important ways. On average, they are much less disadvantaged, and
they garner far more residential loans than areas of other colors. White
neighborhoods are also adjacent to local communities with low levels of

Figure 5.1   Spatial Census Tract Variable Construction Examples

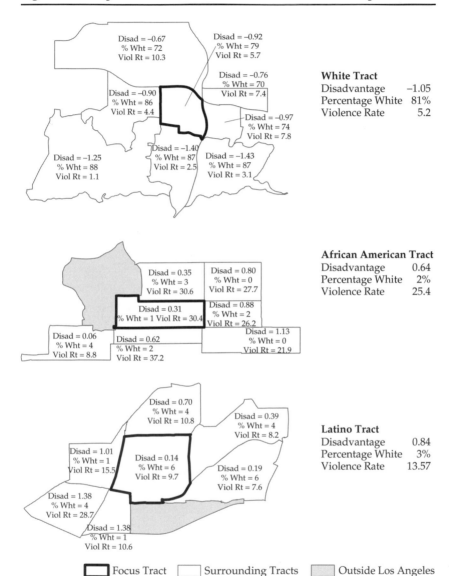

Disad = –0.67
% Wht = 72
Viol Rt = 10.3

Disad = –0.92
% Wht = 79
Viol Rt = 5.7

Disad = –0.76
% Wht = 70
Viol Rt = 7.4

Disad = –0.90
% Wht = 86
Viol Rt = 4.4

Disad = –0.97
% Wht = 74
Viol Rt = 7.8

Disad = –1.25
% Wht = 88
Viol Rt = 1.1

Disad = –1.40
% Wht = 87
Viol Rt = 2.5

Disad = –1.43
% Wht = 87
Viol Rt = 3.1

White Tract
Disadvantage   –1.05
Percentage White   81%
Violence Rate   5.2

Disad = 0.35
% Wht = 3
Viol Rt = 30.6

Disad = 0.80
% Wht = 0
Viol Rt = 27.7

Disad = 0.31
% Wht = 1 Viol Rt = 30.4

Disad = 0.88
% Wht = 2
Viol Rt = 26.2

Disad = 0.06
% Wht = 4
Viol Rt = 8.8

Disad = 0.62
% Wht = 2
Viol Rt = 37.2

Disad = 1.13
% Wht = 0
Viol Rt = 21.9

African American Tract
Disadvantage   0.64
Percentage White   2%
Violence Rate   25.4

Disad = 0.70
% Wht = 4
Viol Rt = 10.8

Disad = 0.39
% Wht = 4
Viol Rt = 8.2

Disad = 1.01
% Wht = 1
Viol Rt = 15.5

Disad = 0.14
% Wht = 6
Viol Rt = 9.7

Disad = 0.19
% Wht = 6
Viol Rt = 7.6

Disad = 1.38
% Wht = 4
Viol Rt = 28.7

Disad = 1.38
% Wht = 1
Viol Rt = 10.6

Latino Tract
Disadvantage   0.84
Percentage White   3%
Violence Rate   13.57

☐ Focus Tract   ☐ Surrounding Tracts   ▨ Outside Los Angeles

Source: Authors' compilation based on the 2000 census (U.S. Bureau of the Census 2007) and ESRI (2006).

Table 5.1   Mean Values for Spatial Variables for Neighborhoods of Different Colors

Neighborhood Characteristic	White Areas	African American Areas	Latino Areas	Minority Areas	Integrated Areas
Disadvantage	−.582	.820	.641	.562	−.045
Residential instability	−.123	−.193	.150	.097	.160
Residential loans (in thousands of dollars)	$20,908	$5,638	$7,925	$10,934	$14,794
Immigrant characteristics	−.375	−.609	1.607	.506	.213
Percentage white	77.16	11.21	13.28	17.81	46.47
Violent crime rate	2.46	10.19	5.50	6.88	4.64
Property crime rate	59.68	83.75	59.03	70.06	71.64

Source: National Neighborhood Crime Study (Peterson and Krivo 2010).

residential instability, but not to as great a degree as African American areas. Not surprisingly given segregation patterns, white neighborhoods are located next to areas with a very high prevalence of other whites. Violent and property crime are also low in areas near white communities. However, they are not as well positioned with respect to immigration as many other neighborhood types. Only African American areas are surrounded by neighborhoods with fewer immigrants. Areas that surround all other types of neighborhoods tend to be worse off (more disadvantaged, more residentially unstable, fewer loan dollars received, and fewer whites) than areas near white communities. As with internal characteristics, the contrast for nearby areas is most extreme when comparing white to African American areas, especially for disadvantage, investments, and crime. The conditions that surround integrated neighborhoods are somewhat more favorable than for African American, Latino, and minority areas for key characteristics like disadvantage, residential loans, and white presence.

Violent Crime

To provide an initial assessment of which aspects of surrounding neighborhoods may be critical in generating differentials in local violent crime, we incorporate the spatial measures of neighborhood characteristics into our model *one at a time.* The results are presented in table 5.2. The values represent the ratios of the neighborhood violent crime rate

Table 5.2   Ratios of Violent Crime Rates for African American, Latino, Minority, and Integrated Versus White Neighborhoods When Accounting for Single Spatial Neighborhood Characteristics

Accounting For:	African American Area/ White Area	Latino Area/ White Area	Minority Area/ White Area	Integrated Area/ White Area
No spatial variables	1.65*	1.29*	1.53*	1.36*
Spatial residential instability	1.64*	1.31*	1.55*	1.34*
Spatial residential loans	1.60*	1.23*	1.51*	1.34*
Spatial immigration	1.68*	1.27*	1.55*	1.35*
Spatial disadvantage	1.49*	1.16	1.41*	1.30*
Spatial percentage white	1.05	0.91	1.08	1.10
Spatial violent crime rate	1.43*	1.21*	1.42*	1.32*

Source: National Neighborhood Crime Study (Peterson and Krivo 2010).
Note: City variables and all other neighborhood factors are controlled in all models (see table 4.1 for the full list of variables).
*$p < .05$

in the average African American, Latino, minority, or integrated area compared to that for the average white area. For the sake of comparison, the first row reproduces the ratios from the analysis that included the full set of *internal* neighborhood characteristics and aspects of city context (see the last row of table 4.2). Even before considering conditions in adjacent neighborhoods, violent crime is an average of 29 to 65 percent higher in nonwhite than in white areas.

The next three rows in table 5.2 present the violence ratios when residential instability, residential loans, and immigration for surrounding areas are individually taken into account. The differential spatial distributions of these three characteristics across varying neighborhoods of color are not important in accounting for race-ethnic inequality in community-level violent crime; the violence ratios of nonwhite to white areas change by at most a very small degree when each factor is added. In contrast, nearby disadvantage and percentage white are important for understanding why violence in nonwhite areas is higher than in white neighborhoods. Violence in African American, minority, and integrated areas would be 49, 41, and 30 percent higher, respectively, than for white neighborhoods if the areas were all similarly situated with regard to disadvantage levels in adjacent neighborhoods. This is a reduction in the violence gap from white areas of about 25 percent for African American and minority neighborhoods and about 17 percent for integrated areas compared to the results with no spatial factors. Disadvantage in adjacent areas is even more important in accounting for higher levels of violence in Latino versus white neighborhoods: the Latino-white neighborhood violent crime differential is 45 percent lower once the disadvantage spatial factor is controlled. This results in a Latino-white gap in violence of just 16 percent, a differential that is not statistically significant.

Proximity to neighborhoods with larger numbers of white residents is even more influential than spatial disadvantage for ethno-racial neighborhood inequality in violence. When percentage white in nearby areas is included, violent crime rates in white neighborhoods are essentially indistinguishable from the levels in all other ethno-racial communities. Violence rates in African American, minority, and integrated neighborhoods are just 5, 8, and 10 percent higher, respectively, than in white communities when the adjacent white population is taken into account. Latino neighborhoods would have almost 10 percent *less* violent crime than white neighborhoods if they were located near areas with as large a white presence. Clearly, proximity to the structural privileges associated with whites is critical in gaining access to the social, political, and economic resources that distance communities from threats to safety and keep violence low.

The final row of table 5.2 shows net race-ethnic differences in violence when the average level of violence in adjacent neighborhoods is controlled, a common practice in past research. Here the violence ratios are similar to those observed when levels of disadvantage in adjacent neighborhoods are included. The violence rate for African American, Latino, minority, and integrated areas is 43, 21, 42, and 32 percent higher, respectively, than in white neighborhoods when violence for adjacent neighborhoods is the sole spatial factor considered. However, the impact of spatial clustering of violence (or any other spatial factor) on race-ethnic inequality in violent crime may result from its connection with locational patterns for other community conditions. To evaluate this possibility we need to simultaneously examine the role of this factor along with the other spatial factors.

Table 5.3 presents results for ethno-racial gaps in violent crime from models that include measures of multiple aspects of the character of surrounding neighborhoods. (Results that do not include spatial factors are presented for comparison purposes.) Four substantive spatial conditions are initially included: residential instability, residential loans, disadvantage, and percentage white. The presence of immigrants in neighboring communities is excluded because statistically it has no relationship with violence. Next we add violence in adjacent neighborhoods. Differences in the violence rates of African American, minority, and integrated areas compared to white areas remain after accounting for the spatial

Table 5.3   **Ratios of Violent Crime Rates for African American, Latino, Minority, and Integrated Versus White Neighborhoods When Simultaneously Accounting for Sets of Spatial Neighborhood Characteristics**

Accounting For:	African American Area/ White Area	Latino Area/ White Area	Minority Area/ White Area	Integrated Area/ White Area
No spatial variables	1.65*	1.29*	1.53*	1.36*
Plus four spatial variables[a]	1.19*	1.01	1.21*	1.16*
Plus spatial violent crime rate[a]	1.13	1.02	1.19*	1.17*

Source: National Neighborhood Crime Study (Peterson and Krivo 2010).
Note: City variables and all other neighborhood factors are controlled in all models (see table 4.1 for the full list of variables).
[a]Spatial variables for neighborhood residential instability, residential loans, disadvantage, and percentage white are included.
*$p < .05$

concentration of the four community conditions (row 2). However, the gaps are relatively modest overall (between 16 and 21 percent) when compared to the scenario where the social and economic character of neighboring areas is not controlled. For African American, minority, and integrated areas, differentials in violent crime from white neighborhoods are 56 to 70 percent lower than observed when no spatial factors are incorporated. Conditions in spatially proximate neighborhoods have even more impact in accounting for higher levels of violence in Latino compared to white areas: the Latino neighborhood excess in violence declines by 97 percent to essentially no difference when spatial factors are considered. Taking violence in neighboring communities into account does not appreciably alter the crime differentials (row 3), although the African American–white gap is no longer meaningful. Thus, the role of nearby violence may result from its connections with the spatial concentration of other community conditions, most notably disadvantage and the prevalence of white residents.

How large are the relationships of the spatial factors with neighborhood violence, and how do they compare with those for their nonspatial counterparts? Table 5.4 presents the magnitudes of influence of the neighborhood internal and spatial factors before and after controlling for levels of violence in proximate areas as percentage changes in violence for a one-standard-deviation unit change in each characteristic.[4] Without controlling for violence in neighboring areas (model 1), we find

Table 5.4   Effects of Neighborhood Internal and Spatial Characteristics on Neighborhood Violent Crime

Characteristic	Percentage Change in Neighborhood Violence	
	(1)	(2)
Neighborhood conditions		
Young males	0.2%	1.1%
Residential instability	22.2*	18.3*
Residential loans	−6.1*	−6.9*
Immigration	−13.2*	−10.7*
Disadvantage (at the mean)	47.1*	46.4*
Spatial neighborhood conditions		
Spatial residential instability	17.7*	10.0*
Spatial residential loans	−2.9	4.1
Spatial disadvantage	8.3*	1.0
Spatial percentage white	−17.5*	−16.1*
Spatial violent crime rate		25.3*

Source: National Neighborhood Crime Study (Peterson and Krivo 2010).
Note: Values represent the percentage change in the neighborhood violent crime rate for a one-standard-deviation unit change in the characteristic. The models include ten city characteristics (segregation, disadvantage, manufacturing, population, percentage African American, percentage recent movers, percentage foreign-born, percentage young males, South, and West).
*$p < .05$

that more disadvantaged and residentially unstable focal areas have more violent crime; rates of violence are lower in neighborhoods with larger immigrant populations and greater home loan investments. As shown before we considered spatial relationships (see chapter 4), levels of disadvantage and residential instability *within* neighborhoods have the strongest connections with violent crime.[5] Still, all internal factors except age-sex composition have statistically meaningful associations with local violence.

Controlling for the influences of internal neighborhood conditions, three characteristics of proximate areas—residential instability, disadvantage, and the percentage of white residents—have important associations with rates of violent crime. Residential instability in neighboring areas has a sizable impact, even though this relationship is not important for race-ethnic differences in violence (see table 5.2). Indeed, residential instability in proximate areas is nearly as influential as instability in the focal community; the spatial and internal area indicators increase the rate of violence by 18 and 22 percent, respectively, per one-standard-deviation unit change in their levels. A similar increase in disadvantage in bordering neighborhoods is associated with about 8 percent more violent crime. Not surprisingly, location near more heavily white areas is strongly connected with violence. For example, a neighborhood that has an average of 30 percent more whites in neighboring communities (one standard deviation unit) will have nearly 18 percent less violent crime.

Does violence in neighboring areas contribute to this type of crime within focal communities? And are the relationships of other spatial factors altered when violence in nearby communities is incorporated? Violence in bordering areas has a strong association with violent crime for focal neighborhoods. Areas with 4.8 more incidents per 1,000 residents in adjacent neighborhoods (one standard deviation) have 25 percent more violent crime. Yet, areas' own social conditions have about the same associations with criminal violence whether or not the spatial violence factor is controlled. This is not the case, however, for some of the spatial characteristics. White concentration in nearby areas remains important over and above its association with levels of proximate violence. But the connections of residential instability and disadvantage in adjacent neighborhoods with area violence are notably reduced. In fact, nearby disadvantage is no longer significantly related to violent crime. Thus, being located near more highly disadvantaged neighborhoods tends to increase violence by intensifying violent crime in neighboring communities. Overall, then, it appears that disadvantage heightens community violence both from dynamics that operate within neighborhoods and from the way the spatial concentration of violence reverberates by affecting violence in nearby areas.

Figure 5.2 clarifies how these findings fit together in accounting for race-ethnic differentials in violence. Here we present predicted rates of violent crime for the five different communities of color with no spatial variables taken into account (bars on left) compared to those with all five spatial factors incorporated (bars on right). The rates in this figure assume that all neighborhoods have the average character of white tracts.[6] Thus, they provide an optimistic scenario where all types of areas hypothetically have the typical character of white communities. What would ethno-racial neighborhood crime patterns look like under this scenario? As can be seen on the left, white neighborhoods have notably less violent crime than all other areas of color even when considered equivalent in city and internal neighborhood conditions.[7] However, the location of areas relative to the substantive character of neighboring communities is obviously important in accounting for these differentials (bars on right). Violent crime would be much more similar in all racially-ethnically distinct types of areas if the character of the communities that

Figure 5.2   Predicted Rates of Violent Crime for Neighborhoods of Different Colors

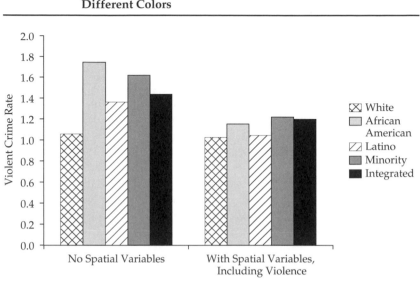

Source: National Neighborhood Crime Study (Peterson and Krivo 2010).
Note: Predicted values hold the city and all other neighborhood characteristics constant at white mean levels.

border them was equalized (and at white levels). Rates of violent crime would vary from just 1.0 per 1,000 population in white neighborhoods to 1.2 in minority and integrated areas.

It is hard to overestimate the importance of this finding. Urban neighborhoods are racially and ethnically divided in ways that form the basis for highly differentiated levels of involvement with violent crime. White neighborhoods benefit from the dual privileges of low internal disadvantage as well as embeddedness within a context of other white and advantaged areas. African American, Latino, and minority neighborhoods suffer a type of double jeopardy. On the one hand, they are at risk of greater violence stemming from their own internal—often highly disadvantaged—character. On the other hand, they bear the brunt of very substantial isolation from violence-reducing structures and processes because they are surrounded by areas with high levels of disadvantage and few whites. Thus, the findings reported here make plain that neighborhood racial composition in itself is not the key to neighborhood differences in violent crime. Rather, segregation into racially distinct communities provides a mechanism for meting out and channeling differentiated societal resources into neighborhoods that are highly unequal in internal character, spatial location, and hence the social problems, like violence, that these produce.

Table 5.5   Ratios of Property Crime Rates for African American, Latino, Minority, and Integrated Versus White Neighborhoods When Accounting for Single Spatial Neighborhood Characteristics

Accounting For:	African American Area/ White Area	Latino Area/ White Area	Minority Area/ White Area	Integrated Area/ White Area
No spatial variables	1.10	1.08	1.11*	1.08*
Spatial residential instability	1.10	1.09	1.12*	1.07*
Spatial residential loans	1.07	1.04	1.09	1.06*
Spatial immigration	1.12*	1.06	1.12*	1.07*
Spatial disadvantage	1.01	0.99	1.04	1.04
Spatial percentage white	0.85*	0.88*	0.91*	0.96
Spatial property crime rate	1.07	1.05	1.08	1.07*

Source: National Neighborhood Crime Study (Peterson and Krivo 2010).
Note: City variables and all other neighborhood factors are controlled in all models (see table 4.1 for the full list of variables).
*$p < .05$

Property Crime

Assessment of how conditions in nearby neighborhoods affect rates of property crime proceeds in the same manner as that just discussed for violence. Table 5.5 provides results from analyses that incorporate each substantive spatial measure one at a time. The first row presents ratios of criminal inequality with only internal neighborhood characteristics and city conditions controlled (from table 4.4). Ethno-racial differences in property crime are nowhere near as great as for violence, averaging just 8 to 11 percent higher in nonwhite and integrated neighborhoods than in white neighborhoods.

Higher levels of residential instability, residential loans, and immigration in bordering areas are not consequential for neighborhood race-ethnic differentials in property offenses (rows 2 to 4). The ratios of white to other area property crime change at most very modestly when each of these factors is taken into account. In contrast, disadvantage in adjacent areas has some impact on property crime differentials. Rates would be the same in white, African American, and Latino neighborhoods if these types of areas were all surrounded by comparable levels of disadvantage. Property offenses would be just 4 percent higher for minority and integrated communities than for white communities, a difference that is not statistically meaningful. Proximity to whites is more important for criminal inequality. Property crime rate ratios would be lower

Table 5.6   Ratios of Property Crime Rates for African American, Latino, Minority, and Integrated Versus White Neighborhoods When Simultaneously Accounting for Sets of Spatial Neighborhood Characteristics

Accounting For:	African American Area/ White Area	Latino Area/ White Area	Minority Area/ White Area	Integrated Area/ White Area
No spatial variables	1.10	1.08	1.11*	1.08*
Plus four spatial variables[a]	0.97	0.98	1.02	1.02
Plus spatial property crime rate[a]	0.95	0.95	1.00	1.01

Source: National Neighborhood Crime Study (Peterson and Krivo 2010).
Note: City variables and all other neighborhood factors are controlled in all models (see table 4.1 for the full list of variables).
[a]Spatial lag variables for neighborhood residential instability, residential loans, immigration, disadvantage, and percentage white are included.
*$p < .05$

for the nonwhite and integrated neighborhoods if they were surrounded by white populations of similar size. This is because location near more heavily white areas reduces property crime rates, and all areas that are not white themselves are relatively distant from high concentrations of whites (see table 5.1). Finally, location near areas with more property offenses does little to reduce the crime ratios relative to the analysis with no spatial factors.

Table 5.6 presents race-ethnic property crime ratios when all of the substantive neighborhood spatial factors are included simultaneously and when property crime in adjacent areas is added. Internal neighborhood and city characteristics are controlled. Once characteristics in the surrounding neighborhoods (the social conditions and property crime) are considered, there are no meaningful differences in rates of property offending across the five types of communities. Clearly, providing a complete story regarding the racialized structural foundations of criminal inequality involves understanding the roles of both internal and external community dynamics.

To illuminate how spatial factors compare to internal neighborhood characteristics in their contribution to neighborhood patterns of property crime, we report percentage changes in rates for a one-standard-deviation unit increase in each condition (table 5.7). Before considering the influence of property crime in bordering communities, all the internal features of neighborhoods except the presence of young males affect

Table 5.7   Effects of Neighborhood Internal and Spatial Characteristics
on Neighborhood Property Crime

Characteristic	Percentage Change in Neighborhood Violence	
	(1)	(2)
Neighborhood conditions		
Young males	–0.6%	–0.2%
Residential instability	24.0*	22.3*
Residential loans	–7.1*	–7.3*
Immigration	–14.8*	–14.3*
Disadvantage (at the mean)	5.9*	4.2
Spatial neighborhood conditions		
Spatial residential instability	10.1*	4.0*
Spatial residential loans	–4.3*	–0.6
Spatial immigration	–1.9	0.9
Spatial disadvantage	13.2*	10.7*
Spatial percentage white	–3.8	–4.9*
Spatial property crime rate		1.4*

Source: National Neighborhood Crime Study (Peterson and Krivo 2010).
Note: Values represent the percentage change in the neighborhood property crime rate for a one-standard-deviation unit change in the characteristic. The models include ten city characteristics (segregation, disadvantage, manufacturing, population, percentage African American, percentage recent movers, percentage foreign-born, percentage young males, South, and West).
$*p < .05$

levels of property crime. Residential instability and immigration have the strongest connections with rates. A sizable increase in residential instability (one standard deviation unit) results in a 24-percent-higher rate of property crime. A similar increase in immigration is associated with nearly 15 percent fewer such crimes. External investments and disadvantage in local communities are also statistically meaningful in affecting the extent to which thefts occur.[8]

For violence, we found that residential instability and percentage white in neighboring areas have the strongest relationships with crime. For property crime, however, adjacent area disadvantage is somewhat more influential than the spatial indicator of residential instability, and proximity to whites is unrelated to property offenses. A standard deviation increase in disadvantage and residential instability in proximate areas results in 13 and 10 percent more theft, respectively. Acquisition of more residential loans in neighboring communities contributes modestly to reductions in property crime. When such offending in nearby communities is controlled,

Figure 5.3   Predicted Rates of Property Crime for Neighborhoods of Different Colors

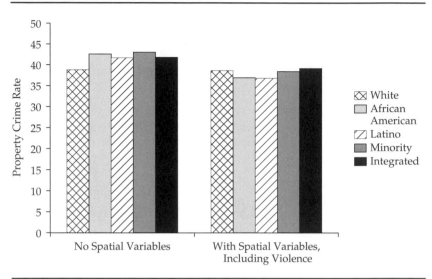

Source: National Neighborhood Crime Study (Peterson and Krivo 2010).
Note: Predicted values hold the city and all other neighborhood characteristics constant at white mean levels.

the influences of adjacent area residential instability, residential loans, and disadvantage are reduced, indicating that these associations operate partially or wholly through the ways in which they modestly increase property offending in adjacent neighborhoods.

Figure 5.3 displays visually how the spatial relationships contribute to inequality in property crime across neighborhoods of different colors. The figure presents predicted rates of property crime for the five race-ethnic community types when no spatial factors are taken into account (on the left) and after adding the spatial variables (on the right). As with violence, we assume that all areas have average white levels for all characteristics. The bars on the left show visually the modest amount of net race-ethnic variation in property crime that exists after we take into account internal neighborhood conditions.[9] On the right, we see that this small amount of differentiation is reduced even more when variation in the spatial character of community locations is taken into account.

Conclusion: Completing the Tale

In this chapter, we have put forth the argument that cross-area relationships are a critical part of the racialized structural sources of differentiation in crime rates. Neighborhoods of varying colors are located in very distinct ways relative to conditions of structural privilege and harm. We asked: does the spatial location of neighborhoods of distinct colors finish the tale of why inequality in crime appears to be so intransigent? The answer to this question is essentially yes. The character of the areas that surround neighborhoods is highly unequal across white, African American, Latino, and other areas. This spatial inequality is responsible for a large portion of the differentials in criminal violence not accounted for by internal neighborhood characteristics. This is also the case for property crime, although net differences across neighborhood types in property offense rates are very modest even before spatial characteristics are considered. In sum, the impact of the racial-spatial divide on race-ethnic inequality in neighborhood crime is both powerful and pervasive across areas within cities.

══ Chapter 6 ══

Conclusion: Implications of the Racial-Spatial Divide

IN CHAPTER 2, we began our discussion with examples of crime rates for racially distinct neighborhoods in two U.S. cities, Columbus, Ohio, and Los Angeles, California. The white, African American, and Latino communities in each of these cities are not far apart physically, but in a manner of speaking, they are worlds apart in their levels of crime. The examples of disparate crime patterns in a few neighborhoods in Columbus and Los Angeles were provided to illustrate the reality of urban life in cities across the United States. Astoundingly, the reasons for this stark variation in crime across white, African American, and Latino neighborhoods, as well as neighborhoods of other colors in U.S. urban areas, have not been addressed within a holistic theoretical framework using sound data. Therefore, throughout this book we have attempted to bring broad perspectives and new empirical evidence to bear in examining this fundamental issue. We are now prepared to summarize our key findings and reflect on the implications of the evidence. In this chapter, we also point out the implications of our results and conclusions for the theoretical perspective we have put forth, future investigations of ethno-racial inequality in crime and related phenomena, and social policies for providing safer neighborhood environments regardless of their racial and ethnic makeup.

Patterns and Processes in Neighborhood Criminal Inequality

The fundamental point of our work is that understanding racial and ethnic differentials in neighborhood crime in the urban United States requires recognition that criminal inequality is a by-product of structural inequality in society at large. In accounting for crime differentials, it is not enough to rely solely on traditional criminological theories, because they often ignore the interconnections of racialized realities with crime-generating conditions. Instead, criminological theories and empirical evidence on the underpinnings of local crime patterns must be integrated with existing knowledge regarding the origins and consequences of the racial order of U.S. society. In this book, we attempted such an integration. We start from the basic argument of race and ethnic scholars that U.S. society is fundamentally structured in ways that serve to maintain white privilege, African American oppression, and a racial hierarchy in which other nonwhite groups generally fall in between. This hierarchy is imprinted in the spatial and social fabric of urban neighborhoods in a pattern that we describe as the racial-spatial divide. This divide is evident in high levels of racial and ethnic segregation, combined with inequalities in a host of critical community resources and disadvantages that result from the separation of unequal groups across neighborhoods. Inequality in the structural conditions of white, African American, Latino, and other communities undergirds the dramatic differentials in crime among these distinct types of areas. From this perspective, differential patterns of crime for ethno-racial groups and neighborhoods do not stem from individual proclivities or a preponderance of "criminals" in an area. Rather, they are the products of structural relations of society.

Data from the National Neighborhood Crime Study for nearly nine thousand neighborhoods spread across eighty-seven cities provide a unique source of information for evaluating arguments regarding the racialized structural sources of neighborhood inequality in crime. Until now, it has been impossible to draw sound, broad-based conclusions about this issue because virtually all prior analyses have been restricted to examination of a small number of places. Looking at a large set of urban areas reveals a stark picture of inequality both in crime, particularly violence, and in the segregated community circumstances that are critical in generating crime. Violence is five times as high for the average African American neighborhood as for the typical white urban community. Further, only about one-fifth of African American areas have violence levels that are as low as those for 90 percent of white areas. Consistent with structural race theories, violence rates are between these levels for Latino, minority, and integrated areas. Rates for these areas are, on average, two and a half to three and a half times those for white communities. Differentials in property offending across the distinct neighborhoods of color are more modest. Average property offense rates are about 30 percent and 50 percent higher for African American than for white and Latino communities, respectively. Mean levels of property offending in minority and integrated areas approach those in African American neighborhoods. Overall, however, there is more overlap in rates across the distinct local areas for property crime than for violent crime.

Differentiation in the structural arrangements that underlie neighborhood inequality in crime is also striking. White, African American, and Latino urbanites often live in separate local areas, and these neighborhoods provide highly divergent social contexts for residents. In the eighty-seven cities studied, 60 percent of whites, 51 percent of African Americans, and 33 percent of Latinos live in areas where the vast majority of their neighbors are of the same race or ethnicity. Thus, residence in segregated neighborhoods is the norm for urban whites and African Americans and is common for Latinos. Further, a full 34 percent of African Americans live in neighborhoods where their separation from other groups is nearly complete, with over 90 percent of residents being members of this same group.

These separate social contexts are starkly differentiated in their socioeconomic character. The story of individual and group racial inequality in the United States is certainly familiar to the readers of this book. Yet the extraordinary differences found across urban neighborhoods of distinct colors are even greater than those observed for individuals. While over 90 percent of white neighborhoods have low poverty, this is the case for only about 25 percent of African American, Latino, and minority areas. Conversely, just 1 percent of white neighborhoods are extremely impoverished, compared to between 15 and 25 percent for African American, Latino, and minority neighborhoods. Integrated areas fall between these extremes. The same basic patterns of ethno-racial differentials favoring whites over all other groups hold for the five remaining aspects of disadvantage (see chapter 3).

Neighborhood inequalities are even more stark when we consider how poverty and other socioeconomic characteristics overlap into a constellation of disadvantage. In fact, the distributions of disadvantage for white and nonwhite neighborhoods could hardly be more dissimilar. African American, Latino, and minority areas are commonly hyperdisadvantaged in that at least four aspects of disadvantage are extremely high. In contrast, virtually no white neighborhoods are hyperdisadvantaged. Furthermore, there is almost no overlap in the disadvantage of white areas with that of neighborhoods of other colors (figures 3.5 through 3.7). White neighborhoods almost exclusively have below-average disadvantage, with an ever-increasing proportion of such areas included at lower and lower levels of disadvantage. African American, Latino, and minority areas have mainly above-average disadvantage, and large portions of these neighborhoods are extremely disadvantaged. The African American case is the most dramatic. A very large proportion of these communities (26 percent) have extraordinarily high disadvantage. Thus, when comparing four types of urban neighborhoods—white, African American, Latino, and minority—the notion of "average" disadvantage is a misnomer. Instead, there is one average for white neighborhoods, reflecting their privileges, and completely different averages for the three types of predominantly nonwhite areas, reflecting their subordinate positions in the urban hierarchy. Integrated neighborhoods provide a clear exception. Levels of disadvantage represent a combination of the character of the white communities and the predominantly nonwhite communities.

Our analyses demonstrate that racialized patterns of disadvantage—and to a lesser degree residential instability, residential loans, and immigration—are central in accounting for variation in crime among neighborhoods of distinct colors. Rates of property offending are very similar across neighborhood types when differences in city and local area conditions are controlled; neighborhood disadvantage makes the greatest contribution to inequality in property crime. Gaps in violent crime rates across types of areas are much larger. Variation in neighborhood disadvantage is also the major contributor to these differentials. However, white privilege in maintaining relatively low levels of violence persists after all of the theoretical and control characteristics are taken into account. The story is essentially the same whether we are considering all neighborhoods or focusing only on areas that are advantaged—that is, areas with low rates of poverty.

Finally, we explored whether the circumstances in the areas that surround neighborhoods are also racialized in ways that help to account for persistent differences in violence across communities. African American neighborhoods are far worse off than white areas in the levels of disadvantage, external investments, and violent crime that are nearby. Other types of areas are intermediate. We also examined the extent to which residing in neighborhoods that are adjacent to predominantly white areas matters for crime levels and criminal inequality. Reflecting segregation, white neighborhoods are surrounded by many whites (an average of 77 percent), and predominantly nonwhite communities (African American, Latino, and minority) are near areas with few whites (an average of less than 20 percent). As with socioeconomic characteristics, integrated neighborhoods have intermediate levels of white representation in proximate areas (mean of 47 percent).

Racialized patterns in the surrounding circumstances are important in accounting for violent crime rates in different types of neighborhoods. Residential instability, disadvantage, and the percentage of white residents in adjacent communities are factors that contribute to neighborhood violence, but only disadvantage and white composition help to account for the observed *inequality* in rates. Also, nearby disadvantage contributes to violence gaps through its influence in heightening violence in adjacent areas. Location near areas with more whites has a very strong impact on levels and differentials in neighborhood violence, even after controlling for the spatial concentration of disadvantage, violent crime, and other characteristics that are internal and external to neighborhoods. Access to the valued social, political, and economic resources and connections that help communities stay safe from violence is apparently facilitated by proximity to areas with large proportions of whites.

As noted, rates of property crime are very similar across distinct ethno-racial neighborhoods after internal community conditions are controlled. Nonetheless, spatial factors are associated with property offending and contribute to the small net differentials in rates. Neighborhoods that have high levels of residential instability and disadvantage nearby have more property crime. This type of offending is less common when larger amounts of residential loans are made in adjacent areas. These effects operate, to some degree, through their impact on property crime rates in contiguous communities. However, only nearby disadvantage and the percentage of white residents are connected with the modest net racial and ethnic differentials in property crime.

The overall story told by the empirical results is that a large racial-spatial divide exists for urban neighborhoods in the United States. This divide is evident in the internal character of neighborhoods, which are highly differentiated across communities with varying racial and ethnic compositions. It is especially large for the critical condition of socioeconomic disadvantage. The positions of neighborhoods of varying colors relative to the areas that surround them also reveal social and spatial divisions across ethno-racial areas. Whether we are examining internal or external conditions, white privilege in residential environments is the norm, as is African American location at the bottom of the hierarchy of local context. The implications of these patterns are clear. The racial-spatial divide that is endemic in urban areas is largely responsible for the dramatic inequalities in crime, particularly violent crime, that exist across urban neighborhoods.

Implications of a Structural Race Perspective

What are the implications of our major conclusion that racialized structures are at the heart of aggregate criminal inequality? The answer to this question is complex, but we find the patterns observed and summarized here to be instructive in a number of ways for theory, research, and policy. Theoretically, we begin with the point that our results show the fruitfulness of drawing on multiple perspectives in theorizing about and examining a complex issue like inequality in neighborhood crime. In developing hypotheses and conducting analyses, we drew on ideas from criminology (especially the role of social disorganization and recent research on inequality in crime across groups and areas), urban sociology (particularly work on the sources and consequences of racial residential segregation in the urban United States, along with arguments about the workings of the macroeconomic context), and racial and ethnic stratification (notably perspectives about the racial organization of society and its consequences). Utilizing these ideas, we offered an integrated perspective on neighborhood criminal inequality in which criminological approaches are embedded within the framework articulated by race scholars and linked with ideas from urban sociology regarding the potential influences of the broader urban context in setting the stage for crime in communities. The findings demonstrate the importance of developing this more holistic understanding of ethnoracial neighborhood inequality in criminal patterns. We examined and demonstrated the importance of the factors that criminologists point to as major structural underpinnings of crime. But as suggested by urban sociologists and race scholars, patterned differentiation in these factors across groups and areas does not occur in a vacuum. Rather, the internal structural conditions of neighborhoods and the circumstances of surrounding areas are fundamentally racialized in ways that specifically reinforce and maintain superiority in the local contexts of whites and widespread deprivation in the contexts of African Americans, Latinos, and sometimes others.

If racialization were not such an integral part of the organization of U.S. society, ethno-racial groups would have more equitable access to societal resources; communities would be less segregated into black, white, brown, and other enclaves; and neighborhoods and adjacent communities would unquestionably be more equal in terms of criminogenic structural conditions like disadvantage, residential instability, and residential loans. In turn, crime in the United States would be dispersed more evenly across communities of different colors. However, the idea of eliminating racialized social arrangements is a mere thought exercise that is not likely to be realized because society is so fundamentally structured to reproduce and maintain race-ethnic inequality. Indeed, the differential resources that flow from the racial order are so beneficial for whites that maintenance of the status quo is its own reward in that whites stay at the top of the hierarchy and gain all of the resources that flow from this position. Conversely, nonwhites, who are so often deeply disadvantaged by the system, have insufficient power and resources to effect substantial change. It is this intransigent organization that makes inequalities in outcomes like crime inevitable. The implications of this structural configuration are particularly troubling because the uneven distribution of crime works to further reproduce racial inequality in a host of arenas. Neighborhoods and groups with more crime are more feared, more avoided, and invested in less often (see Greenbaum and Tita 2004; Liska and Bellair 1995; Liska, Logan, and Bellair 1998). These processes heighten crime, deepen problems of community organization (for example, through incarceration and other criminal justice policies), worsen economic problems, and weaken political clout (Clear 2007; Rose and Clear 1998). Thus, the diminution of ethno-racial criminal inequality is systematically elusive because of the ways in which it feeds back in reproducing its underlying structural sources.

An additional theoretical lesson is that neighborhood ethno-racial differences in crime are the product of circumstances found in places, not of bad people who inhabit them. Often crime problems are attributed to individual agency (see Bobo and Johnson 2004; Young 1991). In other words, a greater prevalence of criminal involvement is blamed on the poor decisions of individual community members. Thus, the heightened criminality found in poor nonwhite areas, with all of the ramifications discussed here, is seen as deserved. However, the systematic nature of the patterns observed and the relationships found in our study render such an interpretation untenable. The dramatic links of neighborhood and neighboring characteristics with very large ethno-racial differentials in violent and property offending make it clear that crime gaps can only be understood through a lens that focuses on how race structures opportunity and community access. Thus, crime is unequal across distinct racial and ethnic neighborhoods, not because of differential proclivities for crime across groups, but because racialization disperses criminogenic structural conditions unevenly.

In applying such a structural race approach, it is critical to understand how segregation, as an organizing principle within urban areas, contributes to crime. As we have shown, segregated white neighborhoods have lower crime because they have fewer crime-generating conditions. This reflects the greater social and economic resources of whites and the greater investments made in areas where whites predominate. In addition, a residentially segregated society is one in which whites have the power to escape the problems that prevail in many other areas of a city. This population faces few barriers to moving from one neighborhood to another, or out of the city altogether. Compared to minorities, whites typically are not limited in where they reside by affordability, discriminatory processes that constrain information about housing, or strong prejudices against having them as neighbors. Greater freedom in residential mobility allows them to continually reproduce their position at the top of the neighborhood hierarchy. When whites move, their superior resources go with them. Furthermore, greater economic and institutional resources from governments, economic investors, and politicians follow the whiteness of communities. Thus, by maintaining segregation, whites are able to escape to communities with few of the circumstances that generate crime and to create environments in which such conditions are rare. This type of white flight has been a major trend in U.S. cities, many of which have lost large shares of their overall and white populations. Our research suggests that this dynamic must be a central part of the theory and analyses of racial and ethnic inequality in neighborhood crime.

Relatedly, we show that white neighborhoods have less crime, not only because of their better conditions (internally and nearby), but also because they are located near areas with more white residents. It is not entirely clear why white prevalence itself would affect levels of crime. However, it is not because there is something inherently superior about living next to white households so that crime problems would be solved by moving nonwhites to areas that are near whites. Racial composition is specifically *not a causal* factor in accounting for crime patterns. Rather, it is a factor connected with the concentration of unequal resources in separate contexts that also produces varied responses from outside actors. If we are to better understand the sources of inequality, we must make a concerted effort to identify all relevant social and structural differentials that are systemically related to community differences in racial composition. In regards to individuals, Eduardo Bonilla-Silva and Tukufu Zuberi (2008, 7) contend that

> we [must] place statistical analysis of race within a historical and social context. It is not a question of how a person's race causes disadvantage and discrimination. The real issue is the way the society responds to an individual's racial identification. . . . Race is not about an individual's skin color. Race is about an individual's relationship to other people within the society.

We agree with this contention and think that it also applies to aggregate units such as neighborhoods. Drawing on this logic, the finding that residence with and near whites is associated with lower levels of crime should be interpreted with regard to the social context and relations that flow to white local areas. We have captured some of these dynamics with indicators of socioeconomic disadvantage, residential investments, the presence of immigrants, and residential instability. However, these factors do not appear to represent all of the status, power, and resource privileges that exist in white areas compared to neighborhoods of other colors. Thus, it is incumbent on researchers to uncover the additional ways in which whites are able to gain privilege for the communities where they reside.

Future Research on the Racial-Spatial Divide

Drawing on a wider array of neighborhoods nested within a larger number of cities than ever before investigated, we have highlighted the significance of the role of racial structure in generating criminal inequality. The NNCS has allowed us to: (1) examine neighborhoods within the context of cities, which is important because characteristics of both types of units have an impact on crime; (2) compare multiple and distinct types of neighborhoods, thus moving beyond only black-white or Latino-black comparisons; (3) consider the positioning of neighborhoods of different colors for an array of socioeconomic conditions, including external resources; (4) incorporate substantive spatial effects; and (5) consider both violent and property crime. Thus, we have avoided a variety of shortcomings of existing research and addressed previously unanswered questions. Now we identify the empirical implications of our work, including the lessons learned and the important questions left unanswered.

First, our analyses showed that much can be gained by comparing neighborhoods across a large number of U.S. cities. Examining diverse types of neighborhoods within relatively homogeneous urban areas, large suburbs, and very large heterogeneous cities like those that have been extensively studied (such as Chicago and Seattle), we demonstrated that it is possible to make meaningful racial and ethnic neighborhood comparisons. By its very nature, U.S. urban racial inequality requires that large sets of neighborhoods be incorporated into research to understand the range of levels of crime and of circumstances that relate to variation in crime across communities of distinct ethno-racial compositions. Otherwise, analysts end up comparing white neighborhoods that are highly advantaged with African American (and perhaps other nonwhite) areas that are heavily disadvantaged. Such comparisons inappropriately combine racial comparisons with economic comparisons. Future analyses must address this fundamental concern in collecting data and continuing to sort out the nature and structural sources of criminal inequality by race and ethnicity.

In addition, examining neighborhoods in a large array of urban areas showed that city context matters for local areas, over and above the character of neighborhoods themselves. For example, neighborhoods in cities that are more segregated have considerably more violence than we would expect from the influence of community race-ethnic composition alone. Thus, everyone in segregated cities pays the price of greater violence. Neighborhood violence is lower in cities that have a stronger manufacturing base, indicating that all neighborhoods reap the benefits of violence reduction from an economy with many stable well-paying jobs. It is impossible to see such influences when studying just a single place because there is no variation in city-level conditions. Only studies like this one that include many diverse cities and neighborhoods provide sufficient variation in context to yield sound conclusions about how city structural conditions affect crime, or other social problems, across the levels that make up the urban system.

A second lesson learned from our investigation is that local areas are connected by external influences in ways that are important for neighborhood crime. This is shown in two ways. We incorporated the dollar amount of residential loans that flow into neighborhoods as an indicator of how much external actors invest in communities. Our analyses showed that areas with more such investments have consistently lower levels of both violent and property crime, confirming the finding from a study of local area crime for Seattle (Squires and Kubrin 2006). Thus, resources that go into communities from outside institutions enhance local environments in ways that are beneficial for creating safer neighborhoods. A high priority for future research is identifying other ways in which community connections with outside institutions and actors bring various resources to local areas that help reduce crime.

The role of external influences on local crime was also shown through the ways in which some aspects of the character of areas that border neighborhoods (residential instability, percentage of white residents, and disadvantage) affect crime. Beyond the substantive import of these findings, we learn that it is empirically important and methodologically possible to incorporate measures of actual spatial conditions that are purported to influence crime. Most past research that has explored spatial influences has examined only the impact on focal neighborhood crime of spatial proximity in the outcome (that is, crime itself). We challenge others to follow our lead and move beyond this approach. In doing so, additional dimensions of adjacent community character should be explored (for instance, wealth, or institutional presence); consideration should also be given to the impact of communities beyond a local area's immediate neighbors to determine whether the reach of spatial influences extends to larger regions within cities. These innovations will help reveal how the dynamic interrelationships among communities play out in ways that significantly enhance problems or keep them at bay.

Third, we have also learned the value of conducting separate and comparative analyses of property and violent crime. Widely examined neighborhood structural conditions are associated with both types of offenses, but there are notable differences in patterns and relationships. In particular, neighborhood disadvantage is more weakly connected to property than violent offenses; none of the city characteristics influence the former, while a number have strong relationships with the latter. These differences cannot be seen when focusing on only one type of crime—most commonly violence—in contemporary neighborhood research. We are not suggesting that entirely separate theoretical explanations for different crimes are needed. However, the dominant focus on criminal violence may blind us to nuanced and important differences across crime types.

Of interest for future work is assessing why the patterns and associations just noted are more muted for property crime than violent crime. Is it because property crimes are more instrumental in character and violent crimes more expressive? Is it that property crime is ubiquitous across cities, which therefore dampens relationships? Does the value of property influence the comparative distribution of this crime across neighborhoods of distinct economic and race-ethnic makeups? In racially and economically privileged areas, do the benefits from theft outweigh its perceived costs such that would-be thieves are not deterred from engaging in such crimes? If so, does this raise both the prevalence and reporting of such crime in white and advantaged compared to nonwhite and disadvantaged communities?

Separate explorations of violent and property crime also provide a more "accurate" picture of ethno-racial inequality in crime. Much of the research on differences in crime has focused on violence, and particularly homicide, which is the gravest but rarest form. Certainly, killings and other serious violent offenses are important crime and public health concerns. But drawing conclusions about ethno-racial neighborhood differentials in street crime from such studies may be misleading. Gaps in property offenses are much less dramatic than is the case for violence. Therefore, basing conclusions on studies of violent offending to the exclusion of property crime may lead to an oversimplified and exaggerated picture of ethno-racial criminal inequality that overstates the criminal involvement of African Americans and other nonwhites and the *lack* of criminal involvement of whites. This is problematic because it feeds into stereotypical images like that of the "criminalblackman" (Quillian and Pager 2001; Russell 1998; Young 2006).

There are also a number of issues for future investigators suggested by our analyses but wholly unattended to here. This book is based on a single snapshot (for 2000) of patterns for neighborhoods in many cities throughout the United States. As a result, we can only speculate about the applicability of the findings across time. Wide-scale social and macroeconomic changes in society, as well as crime trends, may affect relationships and inequalities in ways that are difficult to predict. Our theoretical perspective should be relevant for any time period and across broad social conditions. Without over-time data, however, it is not possible to know how social changes, whether predictable or unforeseen, may affect the processes at hand. Unfortunately, compiling the NNCS for the 2000 period was an extremely time-consuming and expensive process that would not be feasible for routine data collection. We hope that advances in technology will soon make it straightforward for law enforcement and the statistical agencies that supply crime data to compile and distribute such information for neighborhoods in a fashion permitting longitudinal analyses.

Our study also focused exclusively on neighborhoods within large cities (whether central cities, suburbs, or other urban areas) rather than on the full array of neighborhoods spread throughout the central city, suburbs, and outlying areas within *entire* metropolitan regions. This emphasis flowed from the difficulty of obtaining crime data across numerous police jurisdictions. The fact that each metropolitan area is policed by many distinct law enforcement agencies increases the effort involved in collecting information on neighborhood crime by a large order of magnitude. Nonetheless, doing so is critical because some of the important processes that generate criminal differentials across neighborhoods of distinct colors revolve around the ability of whites to move more easily than other groups to neighborhoods spread throughout metropolitan areas. Thus, a priority for researchers should be to obtain crime rates for all the neighborhoods of entire metropolitan areas to examine more completely the dynamics at play in privileging white communities over others. If local data collection efforts become more systematized, movement toward this goal would be facilitated.

A final matter for future investigation is evaluating the processes that underlie the structural relationships we observe. We articulated some of the mechanisms that may link community internal and spatial structural factors to violent and property crime. These include aspects of self-help, strain, and informal and formal social control. Variation in political connections and power, disorder, and ethnic cultures and networks are also potential mechanisms linking local social structure to crime. Yet our data are silent about the relative merits of these and other possible aggregate and individual intervening processes. Additional work that evaluates the social, economic, political, cultural, and other forces that connect structures with criminal and other problem outcomes will advance the understanding of how community conditions are linked to neighborhood crime.

The Project on Human Development in Chicago Neighborhoods (PHDCN), the Los Angeles Family and Neighborhood Survey, and the Seattle Neighborhoods and Crime Project include data on neighborhood processes such as collective efficacy and cultural codes of violence. Studies using these data sometimes show that collective efficacy helps account for the relationship between disadvantage and neighborhood crime (Morenoff, Sampson, and Raudenbush 2001; Sampson, Raudenbush, and Earls 1997). However, these data sets do not allow for examination of the mechanisms connecting inequitable social conditions and neighborhood patterns of crime. As our study has made clear, the racial structure of U.S. society means that single-city studies, such as those noted above for Chicago, Los Angeles, and Seattle, do not have a sufficient number of racially and ethnically distinct but economically similar areas to make appropriate comparisons. Sampson (2009) used data from the PHDCN to demonstrate this point. Thus, researchers need to undertake large-scale, multi-city surveys of neighborhoods and relevant local and extra-local actors to assemble evidence on the mechanisms that produce ethno-racial inequality in crime. Another useful approach would be to conduct comparative qualitative research on a carefully selected set of neighborhoods in different cities. Here the purpose would be to explore in-depth how social processes emerge in similar or distinct ways across communities that are differentiated in their ethno-racial makeup and economic status and located in cities with diverse segregation histories and socioeconomic character.

Policy Implications of Crime and the Racial-Spatial Divide

We believe that we have achieved our main goal of identifying and explaining patterns of property and violent crime across communities with different racial and ethnic compositions. We cannot resist the temptation, however, to comment briefly on proposed policies for reducing or eliminating ethno-racial inequality in crime. Given the racial structure perspective that undergirds the analyses, readers will not be surprised that our recommendations do not focus on the criminal justice system as the solution. As we noted in chapter 2, the institutions making up the criminal justice system are also racialized and, as such, reflect and in many ways support the existing racial order. We certainly appreciate efforts to reduce or eliminate racially and ethnically based disparities in the law, policing, prosecutorial and judicial processing, and criminal punishment. Such steps would make it more likely for minority and disadvantaged citizens to view the system as just. This would thereby encourage their participation in preventing and solving crimes, such that participation would contribute, in turn, to crime reduction in nonwhite neighborhoods. Greater equity in criminal justice arenas could also undermine, symbolically and instrumentally, one of the supporting pillars of the U.S. racialized social structure. Nevertheless, absent a concerted effort to overhaul the entire system, loosely coupled though it is, any movements toward equitable processes and outcomes are likely to yield piecemeal benefits that, however worthy, will not change the fundamental racial structure, even within this single arena.

In line with our theoretical arguments, a key recommendation is to fundamentally alter the deeply rooted social structure that overwhelmingly benefits one group (whites) and harms others (nonwhites). We recognize, however, that such dramatic social change will not be brought about in the short run. Thus, alternative solutions are needed to alleviate the undue burdens of excessive crime and other serious social problems that some groups experience.

Rectifying the extraordinary differences in community conditions across neighborhoods of distinct colors is an obvious direction to take. Local areas in which African American and Latino residents predominate, alone or in combination, are severely lacking in a range of socioeconomic benefits and basic aspects of local infrastructure. These types of areas would clearly profit in many ways from an infusion of critical resources: to alleviate poverty; to bring in jobs and services; to improve educational systems; to fix and upgrade the physical infrastructure of housing, businesses, and public facilities; to increase homeownership and the value of housing; to improve family stability; and generally to increase community well-being. Locating funds to deal with these problems is a serious challenge at any time, but particularly in the current economic context. As we are writing this book, the United States is arguably in the midst of the most severe economic crisis since the Great Depression (Sum et al. 2009). As a result, the prospect of cities being able to fund projects and programs that could bring major changes to troubled minority communities is bleak. Many large cities are strapped for funds to maintain even their most basic services, such as police and fire protection, trash pickup, water provision, and road maintenance. Nonetheless, policymakers should be keenly aware that failure to invest in nonwhite and persistently troubled neighborhoods will only exacerbate the crime and other problems that emanate from constellations of overlapping disadvantages.

Clearly in today's context it is not possible to rely on local governments to develop programs and distribute resources to achieve greater equity across diverse types of ethno-racial neighborhoods. However, as federal officials continue to consider ways to stimulate the economy and set local areas on improved trajectories, special attention should be given to the situations of disadvantaged nonwhite neighborhoods. In the foreword to this book, John Hagan advanced the idea that our finding about the importance of residential loans for reducing neighborhood crime offers a kernel of hope for "counteracting the long-standing and entrenched racial divide that leads to criminal violence." A "sensible and sustained" system of such external investments that are well distributed in minority and economically troubled areas may provide a jumpstart for achieving greater ethno-racial equity in the long run. Thus, we hope that our politicians will consider this possibility as they decide how to handle the current home loan crisis.

Even broader approaches might be considered. For example, a national system of community reparations could be implemented as a strategy for building more equitable residential environments for areas of all colors. This system would not distribute dollars, know-how, and programs to individuals but rather to neighborhoods that have suffered from the long-term historical consequences of a racialized society that harkens back to Jim Crow, slavery, the Dawes Act, and beyond. Another possibility would seek to loosen the links between race, place, and social conditions by "the equalization of opportunities through regional strategies" (powell 2007, 54). With a regional strategy, the metropolitan area is treated as an organic whole, and a regional authority distributes resources and services. Accordingly, all groups and locations within the metropolitan area are served by the same institutional entities regarding housing, zoning, employment, education, public transportation, businesses, and the like. As such, the benefits and pitfalls flowing from these regional authorities would be similar for all metropolitan residents (and organizations). In this way, regionalism should lead to more racially equitable social conditions and, in turn, to lower and more equitable levels of local crime.

Infusions of resources and regionalism are potentially helpful strategies for reducing racial and ethnic disparities in the conditions that promote crime and other important social dislocations. Such efforts, however, will not alter the persistent racial-spatial divide. As noted earlier, the organization of society overall, and of the housing market in particular, gives whites considerable freedom to live wherever they choose (Crowder and South 2005; Rosenbaum and Friedman 2001, 2007; South, Crowder, and Chavez 2005; South, Crowder, and Pais 2008). The privilege of whiteness, coupled with market discrimination and racist attitudes, yields heavily segregated white areas that are distant from the most challenging environments that generate crime. This isolation and distance is highly beneficial for whites, who obtain the substantial benefits of living in neighborhoods and suburban communities that are the safest and richest in resources. Further, when whites are geographically isolated from other groups, they have little vested interest in addressing the underlying structural problems associated with crime (Massey and Denton 1993; Krivo, Peterson, and Kuhl 2009). Therefore, fundamental and lasting reductions in the unequal distribution of crime may not happen until the residential arrangements whereby whites reap undue gains at the expense of nonwhite populations are dismantled.

Race scholars are well aware that policies and programs designed to reduce or eliminate racial disparities in crime and other negative outcomes that are implemented within the current social organization of society can only yield piecemeal change. Notably, community reparations would infuse new resources into neglected minority communities, but they would not change the conditions that allow whites to gain substantially by separating themselves from other groups. The regional approach would address some of the consequences of residential arrangements by bringing all parts of the metropolis into a single system for service, delivery, and regulation. However, this leaves in place racial and class segregation, the social processes that maintain such segregation, and various market and other mechanisms by which benefits flow to white and other high-status areas.

In light of problems with these proposals, some race scholars call for more systemic social and activist strategies to challenge white privilege and the status quo (Bonilla-Silva 2001, 2003; Bonilla-Silva and Zuberi 2008; Zuberi and Bonilla-Silva 2008a). Specifically, they advocate for a new and more militant civil rights movement oriented toward equality of *status* among racial groups. This movement would demand full substantive benefits and refuse to accept second-class citizenship for African Americans, Latinos, and other racial and ethnic minorities. It is beyond the scope of this book to assess how such a movement would be brought about or the circumstances under which it might succeed or fail in achieving equality of status across racial and ethnic groups. However, the role proposed for researchers resonates strongly with us. Race scholars call upon analysts to demythify and deracialize the ideologies (for example, color-blindness, abstract liberalism), policies, and practices that support systems of racial stratification (Bonilla-Silva and Zuberi 2008; Twine and Warren 2000; Zuberi and Bonilla-Silva 2008a, 2008b).

Our decision to conduct this study and write this book was not a response to this agenda. Rather, our motivation has always been to provide as full and accurate a picture of the structural underpinnings of race and ethnic differences in crime as possible. Yet our views and the evidence we present about why there is such a high level of ethno-racial criminal inequality align with those of race scholars. As such, the work reported in this book serves both a demythifying and deracializing function. We identify the ways in which the underlying racial order perpetuates racial disparities in crime. In doing so, we make clear that progress in eliminating these disparities, as well as those for other problems that plague urban areas, depend on systematically exposing and attacking the broad-based racialized structure of U.S. society.

═ Notes ═

Chapter 2

1. In Columbus, only twenty-six tracts (13 percent) averaged one or more murders per year from 1999 to 2001.

2. Note that the rates for Los Angeles do not include rapes; the police department did not provide data for this offense. Rapes constitute a small portion of reported violent crimes at just 0.8 percent in Los Angeles and in the nation as a whole (Federal Bureau of Investigation 2001).

3. Over 40 percent of all deaths of African American males age fifteen to twenty-nine are due to homicide. Over 20 percent of deaths among Hispanic males of these ages are homicides. As a cause of death for white non-Hispanic males, homicide ranks fourth for ages fifteen to nineteen (4.3 percent of all deaths), third for ages twenty to twenty-four (4.6 percent of all deaths), fifth for ages twenty-five to twenty-nine (4.6 percent of all deaths), and fifth for ages thirty to thirty-four (3.6 percent of all deaths).

4. With Omi and Winant's racial formation perspective, both social structure and cultural representations are critical to how race is created, used, reproduced, and changed. Here we emphasize the structural component because of its centrality to our approach and that of others theorizing about racial inequality.

5. These are not the only authors who provide structural theoretical perspectives on racial inequality. Rather, our discussion is intended to illustrate the types of structural theoretical approaches being applied to understand the meaning of race in society. Examples of other noteworthy perspectives include laissez-faire racism (Bobo 2004; Bobo, Kluegel, and Smith 1997) and structural racism (Aspen Institute 2004; Grant-Thomas and powell 2009; powell 2007). Further, we do not mean to deny the distinctions that exist across the views of various race scholars. Rather, we intend to point up the essential commonalities emphasized in structurally based race approaches.

6. For 1960 the Census Bureau reported data for "nonwhites," while for 2007 it provided data for "blacks."

7. As we were preparing this book, the collapse of the subprime market was a serious contributor to the major economic recession that began in 2008. The Obama administration and the U.S. Congress are now developing

policies and legislation to stabilize the housing market and the broader economy.

8. Of additional importance, the direction of influence between preferences for integration and actual behavioral integration is from preferences to actual integration, not vice versa. Indeed, actual neighborhood integration with minorities has no effect on one's preferences for such integration (Charles 2006).

9. Claude Fischer and his colleagues (2004) show that the decline in black-white segregation extends back to 1970.

10. In 1896, *Plessy v. Ferguson* (163 U.S. 537 [1896]) legalized segregation through the doctrine of "separate but equal." Such legalized segregation was not overturned until the 1954 decision in *Brown v. Board of Education of Topeka* (347 U.S. 483 [1954]).

11. Crime under these circumstances represents what Robert Merton (1938) and other strain theorists (for example, Messner and Rosenfeld 2001) describe as innovative behavior.

12. Defining concentrated disadvantage as the top quarter of disadvantage for all U.S. neighborhoods, Sampson and his colleagues (2008) found a higher proportion of white (and Latino) children living in Chicago areas of concentrated disadvantage. However, under this definition, 97 percent of African American children included in their Chicago survey lived in such conditions, again making comparisons impossible.

13. Census tracts are small, relatively permanent statistical subdivisions of a county or statistically equivalent entity delineated by local agencies under U.S. Census Bureau guidelines. They generally include between 1,500 and 8,000 people, with an optimum population size of 4,000. Tracts are designed to be relatively homogeneous with respect to social, economic, and housing characteristics (available at: http://www.census.gov/geo/www/tiger/glossry2.pdf; accessed March 1, 2010). Given their size and design, census tracts are the best available units approximating neighborhoods for which a wide range of data are available throughout the United States. Census tracts can cross city boundaries; the NNCS includes 9,593 tracts that are wholly or partly within the boundaries of the 91 cities. Excluded from the data set are 623 whole or partial tracts with small populations (less than 300) and 303 cases for which the police department provided no crime data. A large portion of the 926 excluded tracts (756, or 82 percent) are partial tracts where only a small area is inside the city, and the majority of these (57 percent) also have zero population. In addition, 164 census tracts are excluded because more than 50 percent of the tract population lived in group quarters such as dormitories, jails, or prisons. We recognize that census tracts do not necessarily correspond to neighborhoods in a socially meaningful sense. However, they are the best local areas for which the required data are available, and they have been used in prior analyses of urban crime (Crutchfield, Matsueda, and Drakulich 2006; Hipp 2007; Krivo and Peterson 1996; Martinez and Nielsen 2006). It is not clear how data for social neighborhoods would alter

the results. However, logic suggests that the patterns and relationships reported in this book would only be stronger if the units analyzed were closer to what residents and outsiders recognize as neighborhoods.

14.   Census population data for 2000 were not yet available at the time the study began.

15.   Arson is not included because police departments do not consistently collect and maintain records for incidents of arson. In many cities, the fire department or other city agency collects such data.

16.   In twenty-six cities, the police department provided crime counts for the census tract in which crimes occurred. In the remaining sixty-five cities, the police provided data for individual crime incidents with addresses for the location of the offense. These incident data were geocoded and associated with their census tract locations to produce crime counts for census tracts. Geocoding hit rates averaged 96.7 percent and ranged from 83.7 percent to 100 percent. Because the data are based on the location of the crime, not the residence of the perpetrator or victim, the offender and the victim may be residents or nonresidents of the tract where the crime took place. As a check on the quality of the data, we compared total agency counts for each of the seven crimes submitted to us by individual police departments with the total agency count for the same crime reported in the FBI's UCR for the given year. If these figures were within ten percentage points of each other, we included the tract counts for that place, crime, and year; otherwise, the data were considered as missing. There is also missing crime data when police departments were unwilling to provide data for a particular type of crime owing to agency policy or laws that prohibited the release of address-based information for crimes involving victims of rape or homicide.

17.   The U.S. census obtains racial identification by asking a respondent what each person in the household is from among the following categories: white; black, African American, or Negro; American Indian or Alaska Native; a range of specific Asian or Pacific Island origin groups; or some other race. Hispanic/Latino identification is obtained through a separate question about whether each person in the household is Spanish/Hispanic/Latino. Thus, Latino-identified individuals can be of any census racial identification.

18.   For a few cities, data were unavailable for one of the three years from 1999 to 2001, but the police were able to provide data for 2002. In these cases, the 2002 data were substituted for the missing year's data. In other cases in which only one or two years of crime data were provided, the three-year count is an estimate derived from the available data. When two years of crime counts were provided, estimates were calculated by multiplying two-year counts by 1.5. When only a single year's crime counts were available, estimates were calculated by multiplying the single year counts by 3. Average annual counts are calculated by dividing the three-year reported or estimated counts of crimes by 3.

19.   Homicide includes murder and non-negligent manslaughter, which is the willful killing of a human being. Robbery involves the taking or attempting

to take anything of value from a person by force or through the threat of force or violence. Burglary is the unlawful entry of a structure to commit a felony or theft. Larceny involves the unlawful taking of property from another, including crimes such as shoplifting, pocket-picking, purse-snatching, and thefts from motor vehicles. Motor vehicle thefts include the stealing of cars, trucks, buses, motorcycles, and the like. Rapes and aggravated assaults are not included in violent crimes because data for these offenses are missing for a substantial number of cities. For rapes, this is mainly due to the refusal of police departments to provide data as a matter of law or policy. Aggravated assault counts are missing mainly because of the poor quality of the data provided (see note 16).

20. All indices are constructed as average z-scores of the variables noted in the text and in table 2A.2.

21. Residential loans include conventional, Federal Housing Administration, and Veterans Administration loans for single- or multi-family home purchases, home improvements, or refinancing.

22. The Index of Dissimilarity has long been the most widely used measure in the study of segregation. However, it taps only one way of thinking about how groups are spread residentially across neighborhoods within cities and can overlook some potentially important aspects of segregation. For example, the value of D will be the same in two places where African Americans are similarly spread across areas whether this population is very small (say, just 1 percent) or relatively large (say, 50 percent). African Americans would have much more potential exposure to whites, however, in the former city than in the latter. Relatedly, African Americans would be much more isolated in terms of how much their potential contacts were limited to other African Americans in the city that is half black. To explore the implications of this issue, we compared the role of D with that of indicators of residential isolation of African Americans and residential exposure of African Americans to whites in all of the statistical models that we discuss later in the book. These show the same patterns as found for D for both violent and property crime. African American isolation contributes to more violent crime but not to property crime. Conversely, African American exposure to whites significantly reduces violent crime but has no relationship with property offending.

Chapter 3

1. Those who are jobless include officially unemployed individuals who are out of work and looking for employment. They also include persons who are out of the labor force, are not employed, and are not looking for work, potentially because they are discouraged and hence have involuntarily dropped out of the labor force. Additional groups who are jobless include those in the prime working ages who are voluntarily out of the labor force because they are homemakers, retired, and the like. The data do not allow us to separate those who are involuntarily out of the labor force from those who are voluntarily out of the labor force. Thus, we include the total non-

employed population in our joblessness rate and restrict the measure to the pre-retirement age group.

2. The 40 and 20 percent cutoffs for this variable are, respectively, approximately one-half of a standard deviation above and below the mean percentage of professional workers for all census tracts in our sample.

Chapter 4

1. Specifically, we fit hierarchical linear models with tracts as level-one units and cities as level-two units (representing tracts as cases that are embedded within cities as contexts). Because we are analyzing relatively rare events within small units, we use a nonlinear Poisson model with crime counts as the outcome variable. We specify that these counts have variable exposure by tract population and thereby make the analysis one of rates. A common concern in the application of the Poisson model is that it assumes equal mean and variance of the dependent variable. However, in the case of rare count events like those analyzed here, this assumption is frequently violated, with the variance being considerably larger than the mean—that is, there is overdispersion (Long 1997; Osgood 2000). In our analyses, we tested for overdispersion and found that it is significant in all models. Hence, we control for overdispersion in the level-one variance. We use HLM 6.06 to fit our multilevel models. In HLM, a Poisson model with overdispersion is analogous to a negative binomial model. Also, the specification in HLM that crime counts have variable exposure by tract population is equivalent to specifying a negative binomial model in which tract population is included as an independent variable with its parameter fixed at 1.

2. This interpretation results from how variables in the models are centered. Specifically, all continuous variables are grand-mean centered.

3. These values are computed as ($[e^{(b \times st.dev)} - 1] \times 100$) for all variables except South and West, which are categorical (Long and Freese 2005).

4. The significance levels of the variables as indicated with the stars were determined based on model coefficients and standard errors, not the percentage change values presented in the table.

5. Interaction terms for African American, Latino, minority, and integrated neighborhoods (white is the reference group) by disadvantage were added to the full model to test for variation in effects because both factors involved are at the same level (neighborhood) in the hierarchical analysis.

6. We recognize that low-poverty neighborhoods are not necessarily comparable on all possible characteristics that might be of relevance to local crime. They may still differ to some degree in their income distributions, the prevalence of high-status workers, household wealth, and the like. Future work should explore in more detail these and other possible confounding differences. Researchers will face one challenge in particular: the more dimensions one tries to simultaneously take into account, the fewer racially distinct and otherwise comparable communities exist.

Chapter 5

1. Tita and Greenbaum's (2009) approach is useful in drawing attention to the substantive mechanisms that underlie spatial effects. However, it relies on techniques that assess only how the outcome, gang violence, is related across space with levels of the same outcome in other areas, rather than measuring the processes that might account for such relationships.

2. While Mears and Bhati's (2006) work points up the importance of the substantive impact of communities on one another, their actual indicators are problematic. They measure resource deprivation in socially similar areas as the weighted average level of deprivation in areas of the city that are the most racially-ethnically comparable to one another. In essence, this measure represents the level of disadvantage in Chicago areas for all heavily black neighborhoods, the level of disadvantage in Chicago for all heavily Latino neighborhoods, and the level of disadvantage for all heavily white neighborhoods. This is problematic for the purpose of understanding how spatial factors may be sources of ethno-racial inequality in neighborhood crime because the social similarity variable combines differences in race-ethnic composition and disadvantage into a single construct. Mears and Bhati (2006) interpret the results as if social similarity, rather than spatial similarity, has a more potent influence on homicide. However, in reality, they have shown that *citywide racial* inequality in deprivation is strongly associated with *local* variation in lethal violence. In addition, to the degree that racially similar neighborhoods are located near one another (a common pattern for African Americans and whites in Chicago), the social similarity deprivation variable overlaps with the spatial proximity measure. This provides an additional explanation of why the latter factor is not found to be important when the two variables are modeled together.

3. These spatial lag variables are computed by multiplying tract characteristic values by a row standardized first-order spatial contiguity matrix (queen criterion). The diagonal of the matrix is filled with zeros, indicating that a tract is not a neighbor of itself.

4. These are the statistical effects for the internal and spatial neighborhood factors from the models for which we presented race-ethnic composition differentials in table 5.3.

5. The relationship of disadvantage in the neighborhood is also stronger at lower levels than at higher ones. As reported in table 5.4, a one-standard-deviation increase in focal neighborhood disadvantage is associated with a 47.1 percent increase in violent crime *at mean disadvantage* (index value of 0). When disadvantage is low (one standard deviation below the mean), a 74.5 percent increase in violence would be expected for the same change in disadvantage. At high disadvantage (one standard deviation above the mean), this value is just 24.1 percent.

6. Specifically, all parameters from the models for which results are presented in table 5.4 are multiplied by the mean white neighborhood values for the variables. To produce the predicted rates per 1,000 population reported in figure 5.2, the products from this multiplication are summed, exponentiated, and multiplied by 1,000.

7. This reflects the quantitative ratios of crime that were presented in the last row of table 4.2, which are also repeated in the first rows of tables 5.2 and 5.3.

8. Disadvantage has a modest association with property crime at its mean level when spatial factors are considered. However, the relationship is stronger when disadvantage levels are low, and it is decidedly weaker at higher levels.

9. This reflects the quantitative ratios of crime presented in the last row of table 4.4, which are repeated in the first rows of tables 5.5 and 5.6.

References

Alba, Richard D., and Victor Nee. 2003. *Remaking the American Mainstream: Assimilation and Contemporary Immigration.* Cambridge, Mass.: Harvard University Press.

Anderson, Deborah, and David Shapiro. 1996. "Racial Differences in Access to High-Paying Jobs and the Wage Gap Between Black and White Women." *Industrial and Labor Relations Review* 49(2): 273–86.

Anderson, Elijah. 1990. *Streetwise: Race, Class, and Change in an Urban Community.* Chicago: University of Chicago Press.

———. 1999. *Code of the Street: Decency, Violence, and the Moral Life of the Inner City.* New York: Norton.

Aspen Institute. 2004. *Structural Racism and Community Building.* Washington, D.C.: Aspen Institute.

Baskin, Deborah, and Ira B. Sommers. 1998. *Casualties of Community Disorder: Women's Careers in Violent Crime.* Boulder, Colo.: Westview Press.

Bean, Frank D., and Gillian Stevens. 2003. *America's Newcomers and the Dynamics of Diversity.* New York: Russell Sage Foundation.

Bean, Frank D., Stephen J. Trejo, Randy Capps, and Michael Tyler. 2001. *The Latino Middle Class: Myth, Reality, and Potential.* Claremont, Calif.: Tomás Rivera Policy Institute.

Beckett, Katherine, Kris Nyrop, and Lori Pfingst. 2006. "Race, Drugs, and Policing: Understanding Disparities in Drug Delivery Arrests." *Criminology* 44(1): 105–37.

Berry, Brian J. L., and John D. Kasarda. 1977. *Contemporary Urban Ecology.* New York: Macmillan.

Beveridge, Andrew A. 2008. "A Century of Harlem in New York City: Some Notes on Migration, Consolidation, Segregation, and Recent Developments." *City and Community* 7(4): 358–65.

Bjornstrom, Eileen E. S., Robert L. Kaufman, Ruth D. Peterson, and Michael D. Slater. 2010. "Race and Ethnic Representations of Lawbreakers and Victims in Crime News: A National Study of Television Coverage." *Social Problems* 57(2): 269–93.

Black, Donald. 1983. "Crime as Social Control." *American Sociological Review* 48(1): 34–45.

Black, Sandra E. 1999. "Do Better Schools Matter? Parental Valuation of Elementary Education." *Quarterly Journal of Economics* 114(2): 577–99.

Blau, Judith R., and Peter M. Blau. 1982. "The Cost of Inequality: Metropolitan Structure and Violent Crime." *American Sociological Review* 47(1): 114–29.

135

Bobo, Lawrence. 2004. "Inequalities That Endure? Racial Ideology, American Politics, and the Peculiar Role of the Social Sciences." In *The Changing Terrain of Race and Ethnicity,* edited by Maria Krysan and Amanda E. Lewis. New York: Russell Sage Foundation.

Bobo, Lawrence D., and Devon Johnson. 2004. "A Taste for Punishment: Black and White Americans' Views on the Death Penalty and the War on Drugs." *Du Bois Review* 1(1): 151–80.

Bobo, Lawrence, James R. Kluegel, and Ryan A. Smith. 1997. "Laissez-Faire Racism: The Crystallization of a Kinder, Gentler, Antiblack Ideology." In *Racial Attitudes in the 1990s: Continuity and Change,* edited by Steven A. Tuch and Jack K. Martin. Westport, Conn.: Praeger.

Bobo, Lawrence, and Camille L. Zubrinsky. 1996. "Attitudes on Residential Integration: Perceived Status Differences, Mere In-Group Preference, or Racial Prejudice?" *Social Forces* 74(3): 883–909.

Bond, Carolyn, and Richard Williams. 2007. "Residential Segregation and the Transformation of Home Mortgage Lending." *Social Forces* 86(2): 671–98.

Bonilla-Silva, Eduardo. 2001. *White Supremacy and Racism in the Post–Civil Rights Era.* Boulder, Colo.: Lynne Rienner Publishers.

———. 2003. *Racism Without Racists: Color-Blind Racism and the Persistence of Racial Inequality in the United States.* New York: Rowman and Littlefield.

Bonilla-Silva, Eduardo, and Karen S. Glover. 2004. " 'We Are All Americans': The Latin Americanization of Race Relations in the United States." In *The Changing Terrain of Race and Ethnicity,* edited by Maria Krysan and Amanda E. Lewis. New York: Russell Sage Foundation.

Bonilla-Silva, Eduardo, and Tukufu Zuberi. 2008. "Toward a Definition of White Logic and White Methods." In *White Logic, White Methods: Racism and Methodology,* edited by Tukufu Zuberi and Eduardo Bonilla-Silva. New York: Rowman and Littlefield.

Bortner, M. A., Marjorie Zatz, and Darnell F. Hawkins. 2000. "Race and Transfer: Empirical Research and Social Context." In *The Changing Borders of Juvenile Justice: Transfer of Adolescents to the Criminal Court,* edited by Jeffrey Fagan and Franklin E. Zimring. Chicago: University of Chicago Press.

Bourgois, Philippe I. 1995. *In Search of Respect: Selling Crack in El Barrio.* New York: Cambridge University Press.

Browning, Christopher R. 2009. "Illuminating the Downside of Social Capital: Negotiated Coexistence, Property Crime, and Disorder in Urban Neighborhoods." *American Behavioral Scientist* 52(11): 1556–78.

Browning, Christopher R., Reginald Byron, Catherine A. Calder, Lauren J. Krivo, Mei-Po Kwan, Jae-Yong Lee, and Ruth D. Peterson. 2010. "Commercial Density, Residential Concentration, and Crime: Land Use Patterns and Violence in Neighborhood Context." *Journal of Research in Crime and Delinquency* (May 2010).

Browning, Christopher R., Seth L. Feinberg, and Robert Dietz. 2004. "The Paradox of Social Organization: Networks, Collective Efficacy, and Violent Crime in Urban Neighborhoods." *Social Forces* 83(2): 503–34.

Bursik, Robert J., Jr., and Harold G. Grasmick. 1993. *Neighborhoods and Crime: The Dimensions of Effective Community Control.* New York: Lexington.

Cancino, Jeffrey M., Ramiro Martinez Jr., and Jacob I. Stowell. 2009. "The Impact of Neighborhood Context on Intragroup and Intergroup Robbery: The San Antonio Experience." *Annals of the American Academy of Political and Social Science* 623(1): 12–24.

Carr, James H., and Nandinee K. Kutty. 2008. *Segregation: The Rising Costs for America.* New York: Routledge.

Carr, Patrick J. 2005. *Clean Streets: Controlling Crime, Maintaining Order, and Building Community Activism.* New York: New York University Press.

Carr, Patrick J., Laura Napolitano, and Jessica Keating. 2007. "We Never Call the Cops and Here Is Why: A Qualitative Examination of Legal Cynicism in Three Philadelphia Neighborhoods." *Criminology* 45(2): 445–80.

Chan, Wendy, and Kiran Mirchandani, eds. 2002. *Crimes of Colour: Racialization and the Criminal Justice System in Canada.* Peterborough, Ontario: Broadview Press.

Charles, Camille Zubrinsky. 2000. "Neighborhood Racial-Composition Preferences: Evidence from a Multiethnic Metropolis." *Social Problems* 47(3): 379–407.

———. 2003. "The Dynamics of Racial Residential Segregation." *Annual Review of Sociology* 29(1): 167–207.

———. 2006. *Won't You Be My Neighbor? Race, Class, and Residence in Los Angeles.* New York: Russell Sage Foundation.

———. 2007. "Comfort Zones: Immigration, Acculturation, and the Neighborhood Racial Composition Preferences of Latinos and Asians." *Du Bois Review* 4(1): 41–77.

Chen, Elsa Y. 2008. "The Liberation Hypothesis and Racial and Ethnic Disparities in the Application of California's Three Strikes Law." *Journal of Ethnicity in Criminal Justice* 6(2): 83–102.

Clear, Todd R. 2007. *Imprisoning Communities: How Mass Incarceration Makes Disadvantaged Neighborhoods Worse.* New York: Oxford University Press.

Cohen, Jacqueline, and George Tita. 1999a. "Editor's Introduction." *Journal of Quantitative Criminology* 15(4): 373–78.

———. 1999b. "Diffusion in Homicide: Exploring a General Method for Detecting Spatial Diffusion Processes." *Journal of Quantitative Criminology* 15(4): 451–93.

Condron, Dennis J., and Vincent J. Roscigno. 2003. "Disparities Within: Unequal Spending and Achievement in an Urban School District." *Sociology of Education* 76(1): 18–26.

Conley, Dalton. 1999. *Being Black, Living in the Red: Race, Wealth, and Social Policy in America.* Berkeley: University of California Press.

Conrad, Cecilia A. 2001. "Racial Trends in Labor Market Access and Wages: Women." In *America Becoming: Racial Trends and Their Consequences,* vol. 2, edited by Neil J. Smelser, William Julius Wilson, and Faith Mitchell. Washington, D.C.: National Academies Press.

Crowder, Kyle, and Scott J. South. 2005. "Race, Class, and Changing Patterns of Migration Between Poor and Nonpoor Neighborhoods." *American Journal of Sociology* 110(6): 1715–63.

Crutchfield, Robert D. 1989. "Labor Stratification and Violent Crime." *Social Forces* 68(2): 489–512.

Crutchfield, Robert D., Ann Glusker, and George S. Bridges. 1999. "A Tale of Three Cities: Labor Markets and Homicide." *Sociological Focus* 32(1): 65–83.

Crutchfield, Robert D., Ross L. Matsueda, and Kevin Drakulich. 2006. "Race, Labor Markets, and Neighborhood Violence." In *The Many Colors of Crime: Inequalities of Race, Ethnicity, and Crime in America,* edited by Ruth D. Peterson, Lauren J. Krivo, and John Hagan. New York: New York University Press.

Dawson, Michael. 1994. *Behind the Mule: Race and Class in African-American Politics.* Princeton, N.J.: Princeton University Press.

de Haan, Willem, and Jan Nijboer. 2005. "Youth Violence and Self-Help." *European Journal of Crime, Criminal Law, and Criminal Justice* 13(1): 75–88.

Delgado, Richard. 2009. "The Law of the Noose: A History of Latino Lynchings." *Harvard Civil Rights–Civil Liberties Law Review* 44(2): 297–313.

Delgado, Richard, and Jean Stefancic. 2001. *Critical Race Theory: An Introduction.* New York: New York University Press.

Denton, Nancy A. 1994. "Are African Americans Still Hypersegregated?" In *Residential Apartheid: The American Legacy,* edited by Robert D. Bullard, J. Eugene Grigsby III, and Charles Lee. Los Angeles: CAAS Publications.

Dodoo, F. Nij-Amoo, and Patricia Kasari. 1995. "Race and Female Occupational Location in America." *Journal of Black Studies* 25(4): 465–474.

Du Bois, W. E. B. 1973. *The Philadelphia Negro: A Social Study.* Philadelphia: University of Pennsylvania Press. (Orig. pub. in 1899.)

Edwards, Korie. 2008. *The Elusive Dream: The Power of Race in Interracial Churches.* New York: Oxford University Press.

Ehlers, Scott, Vincent Schiraldi, and Eric Lotke. 2004. *Racial Divide: An Examination of the Impact of California's Three Strikes Law on African-Americans and Latinos.* Washington, D.C.: Justice Policy Institute. Available at: http://www.justicepolicy.org/images/upload/04-10_TAC_CARacialDivide_AC-RD.pdf (accessed December 21, 2009).

ESRI. 2006. *Data & Maps and StreetMap U.S.A.* [DVD]. Redlands, Calif.: ESRI.

Fagan, Jeffrey, and Franklin E. Zimring, eds. 2000. *The Changing Borders of Juvenile Justice: Transfer of Adolescents to the Criminal Court.* Chicago: University of Chicago Press.

Farley, Reynolds, Mick Couper, and Maria Krysan. 2007. "Race and Revitalization in the Rust Belt: A Motor City Story." Research report 07-620. Ann Arbor: University of Michigan, Population Studies Center (April). Available at: http://www.psc.isr.umich.edu/pubs/pdf/rr07-620.pdf (accessed March 15, 2009).

Farley, Reynolds, Howard Schuman, Suzanne Bianchi, Diane Colasanto, and Shirley Hatchett. 1978. "Chocolate City, Vanilla Suburbs: Will the Trend Toward Racially Separate Communities Continue?" *Social Science Research* 7(4): 319–44.

Farley, Reynolds, Charlotte Steeh, Maria Krysan, Tara Jackson, and Keith Reeves. 1994. "Stereotypes and Segregation: Neighborhoods in the Detroit Area." *American Journal of Sociology* 100(3): 750–80.

Feagin, Joe R. 2000. *Racist America: Roots, Current Realities, and Future Reparations.* New York: Routledge.

Federal Bureau of Investigation (FBI). 2001. *Crime in the United States, 2000: Uniform Crime Reports,* tables 1 and 8. Available at: http://www.fbi.gov/ucr/cius_00/00crime213.pdf (accessed May 28, 2009).

Federal Financial Institutions Examination Council. 2001. *Home Mortgage Disclosure Act Raw Data 2000.* Washington: Federal Reserve System.

Figlio, David N., and Maurice E. Lucas. 2002. "What's in a Grade? School Report Cards and House Prices." Available at: http://bear.cba.ufl.edu/figlio/house 0502.pdf (accessed March 13, 2009).

Fischer, Claude S., Gretchen Stockmayer, Jon Stiles, and Michael Hout. 2004. "Distinguishing the Geographic Levels and Social Dimensions of U.S. Metropolitan Segregation, 1960–2000." *Demography* 41(1): 37–59.

Flippen, Chenoa. 2004. "Unequal Returns to Housing Investments? A Study of Real Housing Appreciation Among Black, White, and Hispanic Households." *Social Forces* 82(4): 1523–51.

Forman, Tyrone A., and Amanda E. Lewis. 2006. "Racial Apathy and Hurricane Katrina: The Social Anatomy of Prejudice in the Post–Civil Rights Era." *Du Bois Review* 3(1): 175–202.

Freeman, Lance. 2006. *There Goes the 'Hood: Views of Gentrification from the Ground Up*. Philadelphia: Temple University Press.

Geolytics. 2003. *Neighborhood Change Database (NCDB)*. East Brunswick, N.J.: Geolytics, Inc.

Gilliam, Franklin D., Jr., and Shanto Iyengar. 2000. "Prime Suspects: The Influence of Local Television News on the Viewing Public." *American Journal of Political Science* 44(3): 560–73.

Gilliam, Franklin D., Jr., Nicholas A. Valentino, and Matthew N. Beckmann. 2002. "Where You Live and What You Watch: The Impact of Racial Proximity and Local Television News on Attitudes About Race and Crime." *Political Research Quarterly* 55(4): 755–80.

Goffman, Alice. 2009. "On the Run: Wanted Men in a Philadelphia Ghetto." *American Sociological Review* 74(3): 339–57.

Gonzales-Day, Ken. 2006. *Lynching in the West: 1850–1935*. Durham, N.C.: Duke University Press.

Gotham, Kevin Fox. 2002a. "Beyond Invasion and Succession: School Segregation, Real Estate Blockbusting, and the Political Economy of Neighborhood Racial Transition." *City and Community* 1(1): 83–111.

———. 2002b. *Race, Real Estate, and Uneven Development: The Kansas City Experience, 1900–2000*. Albany: State University of New York Press.

Grant-Thomas, Andrew, and john a. powell. 2009. "Structural Racism and Color Lines in the United States." In *Twenty-First-Century Color Lines: Multiracial Change in Contemporary America*, edited by Andrew Grant-Thomas and Gary Orfield. Philadelphia: Temple University Press.

Greenbaum, Robert T., and George E. Tita. 2004. "The Impact of Violence Surges on Neighborhood Business Activity." *Urban Studies* 41(13): 2495–2514.

Greene, Judith, Kevin Pranis, and Jason Ziedenberg. 2006. *Disparity by Design: How Drug-Free Zone Laws Impact Racial Disparity—and Fail to Protect Youth*. Washington, D.C.: Justice Policy Institute. Available at: http://www.justice policy.org/images/upload/06-03_REP_DisparitybyDesign_DP-JJ-RD.pdf (accessed December 21, 2009).

Hagan, John, Gerd Hefler, Gabriele Classen, Klaus Boehnke, and Hans Merkens. 1998. "Subterranean Sources of Subcultural Delinquency Beyond the American Dream." *Criminology* 36(2): 309–42.

Hagan, John, Carla Shedd, and Monique R. Payne. 2005. "Race, Ethnicity, and Youth Perceptions of Criminal Injustice." *American Sociological Review* 70(3): 381–407.

Hawley, Amos. 1950. *Human Ecology*. New York: Ronald.

———. 1981. *Urban Society: An Ecological Approach*, 2d ed. New York: Wiley.

Haynes, Bruce. 2008. "The Ghetto: Origins, History, Discourse." *City and Community* 7(4): 347–52.

Heitgerd, Janet L., and Robert J. Bursik Jr. 1987. "Extracommunity Dynamics and the Ecology of Delinquency." *American Journal of Sociology* 92(4): 775–87.

Hipp, John R. 2007. "Income Inequality, Race, and Place: Does the Distribution of Race and Class Within Neighborhoods Affect Crime Rates?" *Criminology* 45(3): 665–98.

Hirsch, Arnold R. 1983. *Making the Second Ghetto: Race and Housing in Chicago, 1940–1960*. New York: Cambridge University Press.

Holzer, Harry J. 2001. "Racial Differences in Labor Market Outcomes Among Men." In *America Becoming: Racial Trends and Their Consequences*, vol. 2, edited by Neil J. Smelser, William Julius Wilson, and Faith Mitchell. Washington, D.C.: National Academies Press.

Hurwitz, Jon, and Mark Peffley. 1997. "Public Perceptions of Race and Crime: The Role of Racial Stereotypes." *American Journal of Political Science* 41(2): 375–401.

Iceland, John. 2009. *Where We Live Now: Immigration and Race in the United States*. Berkeley: University of California Press.

Jackson, Kenneth T. 1985. *Crabgrass Frontier: The Suburbanization of the United States*. New York: Oxford University Press.

Jacobs, Jerry A. 2001. "Evolving Patterns of Sex Segregation." In *Sourcebook on Labor Markets: Evolving Structures and Processes*, edited by Ivar Berg and Arne Kalleberg. New York: Kluwer Academic/Plenum.

Jargowsky, Paul A. 1997. *Poverty and Place: Ghettos, Barrios, and the American City*. New York: Russell Sage Foundation.

———. 2003. *Stunning Progress, Hidden Problems: The Dramatic Decline of Concentrated Poverty in the 1990s*. Washington, D.C.: Brookings Institution Press.

Jargowsky, Paul A., and Mary Jo Bane. 1990. "Ghetto Poverty: Basic Questions." In *Inner-City Poverty in the United States*, edited by Lawrence E. Lynn Jr. and Michael G. H. McGeary. Washington, D.C.: National Academies Press.

———. 1991. "Ghetto Poverty in the United States, 1970–1980." In *The Urban Underclass*, edited by Christopher Jencks and Paul E. Peterson. Washington, D.C.: Brookings Institution Press.

Jiwani, Yasmin. 2002. "The Criminalization of 'Race,' the Racialization of Crime." In *Crimes of Colour: Racialization and the Criminal Justice System in Canada*, edited by Wendy Chan and Kiran Mirchandani. Peterborough, Ontario: Broadview Press.

Johnson, Heather Beth, and Thomas M. Shapiro. 2003. "Good Neighborhoods, Good Schools: Race and the 'Good Choices' of White Families." In *White Out: The Continuing Significance of Race*, edited by Ashley W. Doane and Eduardo Bonilla-Silva. New York: Routledge.

Jones, Nikki. 2009. *Between Good and Ghetto: African American Girls and Inner-City Violence*. Piscataway, N.J.: Rutgers University Press.

Karafin, Diana L. 2009. "Patterns and Consequences of Long-Term Racial and Ethnic Integration in U.S. Metropolitan Neighborhoods." Ph.D. diss., Ohio State University.

Kaufman, Robert L. 2001. "Race and Labor Market Segmentation." In *Sourcebook on Labor Markets: Evolving Structures and Processes,* edited by Ivar Berg and Arne L. Kalleberg. New York: Kluwer Academic/Plenum.

———. 2010. *Race, Gender, and the Labor Market: Inequalities at Work.* Boulder, Colo.: Lynne Rienner Publishers.

Kelling, George L., and Catherine M. Coles. 1996. *Fixing Broken Windows: Restoring Order and Reducing Crime in Our Communities.* New York: Martin Kessler Books.

King, Mary C. 1992. "Occupational Segregation by Race and Gender, 1940–1988." *Monthly Labor Review* 115(4): 30–37.

Kornhauser, Ruth Rosner. 1978. *Social Sources of Delinquency: An Appraisal of Analytic Models.* Chicago: University of Chicago Press.

Krivo, Lauren J., and Robert L. Kaufman. 1999. "How Low Can It Go? Declining Black-White Segregation in a Multiethnic Context." *Demography* 36(1): 93–109.

———. 2004. "Housing and Wealth Inequality: Race-Ethnic Differences in Home Equity in the United States." *Demography* 41(3): 585–605.

Krivo, Lauren J., and Ruth D. Peterson. 1996. "Extremely Disadvantaged Neighborhoods and Urban Crime." *Social Forces* 75(2): 619–50.

———. 2000. "The Structural Context of Homicide: Accounting for Racial Differences in Process." *American Sociological Review* 65(4): 547–59.

———. 2004. "Labor Market Conditions and Violent Crime Among Youth and Adults." *Sociological Perspectives* 47(4): 485–505.

Krivo, Lauren J., Ruth D. Peterson, and Diana Karafin. 2006. "Perceptions of Neighborhood Problems in Racially and Economically Distinct Neighborhoods." In *The Many Colors of Crime: Inequalities of Race, Ethnicity, and Crime in America,* edited by Ruth D. Peterson, Lauren J. Krivo, and John Hagan. New York: New York University Press.

Krivo, Lauren J., Ruth D. Peterson, and Danielle P. Kuhl. 2009. "Segregation, Racial Structure, and Neighborhood Violent Crime." *American Journal of Sociology* 114(6): 1765–1802.

Krivo, Lauren J., Ruth D. Peterson, Helen Rizzo, and John R. Reynolds. 1998. "Race, Segregation, and the Concentration of Disadvantage: 1980–1990." *Social Problems* 45(1): 61–80.

Krysan, Maria. 2002a. "Community Undesirability in Black and White: Examining Racial Residential Preferences Through Community Perceptions." *Social Problems* 49(4): 521–43.

———. 2002b. "Whites Who Say They'd Flee: Who Are They, and Why Would They Leave?" *Demography* 39(4): 675–96.

Krysan, Maria, and Michael Bader. 2007. "Perceiving the Metropolis: Seeing the City Through a Prism of Race." *Social Forces* 86(2): 699–733.

Krysan, Maria, Reynolds Farley, and Mick P. Couper. 2008. "In the Eye of the Beholder: Racial Beliefs and Residential Segregation." *Du Bois Review* 5(1): 5–26.

Kubrin, Charis E., and Tim Wadsworth. 2003. "Identifying the Structural Correlates of African-American Killings: What Can We Learn from Data Disaggregation?" *Homicide Studies* 7(1): 3–35.

Lacy, Karyn R. 2007. *Blue-Chip Black: Race, Class, and Status in the New Black Middle Class.* Berkeley: University of California Press.

LaFree, Gary. 1998. *Losing Legitimacy: Street Crime and the Decline of Social Institutions in America.* Boulder, Colo.: Westview Press.

Lee, Matthew R., and Ramiro Martinez Jr. 2002. "Social Disorganization Revisited: Mapping the Recent Immigration and Black Homicide Relationship in Northern Miami." *Sociological Focus* 35(4): 363–80.

Lee, Matthew T., Ramiro Martinez Jr., and Richard Rosenfeld. 2001. "Does Immigration Increase Homicide? Negative Evidence from Three Border Cities." *Sociological Quarterly* 42(4): 559–80.

Lewis, Amanda E. 2003. *Race in the Schoolyard: Negotiating the Color Line in Classrooms and Communities.* New Brunswick, N.J.: Rutgers University Press.

Lewis Mumford Center for Comparative Urban and Regional Research. 2009. *Segregation Indices for Cities, 2000.* Albany, New York: The University at Albany. Available at: http://mumford.albany.edu/census/WholePop/WPdownload.html (accessed March 3, 2010).

Light, Ivan, and Elsa von Scheven. 2008. "Mexican Migration Networks in the United States, 1980–2000." *International Migration Review* 42(3): 704–28.

Liska, Allen E., and Paul E. Bellair. 1995. "Violent-Crime Rates and Racial Composition: Convergence over Time." *American Journal of Sociology* 101(3): 578–610.

Liska, Allen E., John R. Logan, and Paul E. Bellair. 1998. "Race and Violent Crime in the Suburbs." *American Sociological Review* 63(1): 27–38.

Logan, John R., and Harvey L. Molotch. 1987. *Urban Fortunes: The Political Economy of Place.* Berkeley: University of California Press.

Logan, John R., and Brian J. Stults. 1999. "Racial Differences in Exposure to Crime: The City and Suburbs of Cleveland in 1990." *Criminology* 37(2): 251–76.

Logan, John R., Brian J. Stults, and Reynolds Farley. 2004. "Segregation of Minorities in the Metropolis: Two Decades of Change." *Demography* 41(1): 1–22.

Long, J. Scott. 1997. *Regression Models for Categorical and Limited Dependent Variables.* Thousand Oaks, Calif.: Sage Publications.

Long, J. Scott, and Jeremy Freese. 2005. *Regression Models for Categorical and Limited Dependent Variables with Stata,* 2d ed. College Station, Tex.: Stata Press.

Manza, Jeff, and Christopher Uggen. 2006. *Locked Out: Felon Disenfranchisement and American Democracy.* New York: Oxford University Press.

Marable, Manning. 2003. *The Great Wells of Democracy: The Meaning of Race in American Life.* Cambridge, Mass.: BasicCivitas.

———. 2004. "The Political and Theoretical Contexts of the Changing Racial Terrain." In *The Changing Terrain of Race and Ethnicity,* edited by Maria Krysan and Amanda E. Lewis. New York: Russell Sage Foundation.

———. 2007. "Racializing Justice, Disenfranchising Lives: Toward an Antiracist Criminal Justice." In *Racializing Justice, Disenfranchising Lives: The Racism, Criminal Justice, and Law Reader,* edited by Manning Marable, Ian Steinberg, and Keesha Middlemass. New York: Palgrave Macmillan.

Marable, Manning, Ian Steinberg, and Keesha Middlemass, eds. 2007. *Racializing Justice, Disenfranchising Lives: The Racism, Criminal Justice, and Law Reader.* New York: Palgrave Macmillan.

Martinez, Ramiro, Jr. 2002. *Latino Homicide: Immigration, Violence, and Community.* New York: Routledge Press.

————. 2006. "Coming to America: The Impact of the New Immigration on Crime." In *Immigration and Crime: Race, Ethnicity, and Violence*, edited by Ramiro Martinez Jr. and Abel Valenzuela Jr. New York: New York University Press.

Martinez, Ramiro, Jr., and Amie L. Nielsen. 2006. "Extending Ethnicity and Violence Research in a Multiethnic City: Haitian, African American, and Latino Nonlethal Violence." In *The Many Colors of Crime: Inequalities of Race, Ethnicity and Crime in America*, edited by Ruth D. Peterson, Lauren J. Krivo, and John Hagan. New York: New York University Press.

Martinez, Ramiro, Jr., Jacob I. Stowell, and Jeffrey Cancino. 2008. "A Tale of Two Border Cities: Immigration, Ethnicity, and Homicide." *Social Science Quarterly* 89(1): 1–16.

Massey, Douglas S. 1995. "Getting Away with Murder: Segregation and Violent Crime in Urban America." *University of Pennsylvania Law Review* 143(5): 1203–32.

Massey, Douglas S., Rafael Alarcón, Jorge Durand, and Humberto González. 1987. *Return to Aztlan: The Social Process of International Migration from Western Mexico*. Berkeley: University of California Press.

Massey, Douglas S., Gretchen A. Condran, and Nancy A. Denton. 1987. "The Effect of Residential Segregation on Black Social and Economic Well-being." *Social Forces* 66(1): 29–56.

Massey, Douglas S., and Nancy A. Denton. 1993. *American Apartheid: Segregation and the Making of the Underclass*. Cambridge, Mass.: Harvard University Press.

Massey, Douglas S., and Mitchell L. Eggers. 1990. "The Ecology of Inequality: Minorities and the Concentration of Poverty, 1970–1980." *American Journal of Sociology* 95(5): 1153–88.

Massey, Douglas S., and Mary J. Fischer. 2000. "How Segregation Concentrates Poverty." *Ethnic and Racial Studies* 23(4): 670–91.

Massey, Douglas S., and Shawn M. Kanaiaupuni. 1993. "Public Housing and the Concentration of Poverty." *Social Science Quarterly* 74(1): 109–22.

Matsueda, Ross L., and Kevin Drakulich. 2009. "Perceptions of Criminal Injustice, Symbolic Racism, and Racial Politics." *Annals of the American Academy of Political and Social Science* 623(1): 163–78.

Mauer, Marc. 2009. *The Changing Racial Dynamics of the War on Drugs*. Washington, D.C.: The Sentencing Project. Available at: http://www.sentencingproject.org/doc/dp_raceanddrugs.pdf (accessed December 20, 2009).

McKoy, Deborah L., and Jeffrey M. Vincent. 2008. "Housing and Education: The Inextricable Link." In *Segregation: The Rising Costs for America*, edited by James H. Carr and Nandinee K. Kutty. New York: Routledge.

McNulty, Thomas L. 2001. "Assessing the Race-Violence Relationship at the Macro Level: The Assumption of Racial Invariance and the Problem of Restricted Distributions." *Criminology* 39(2): 467–90.

McNulty, Thomas, and Steven R. Holloway. 2000. "Race, Crime, and Public Housing in Atlanta: Testing a Conditional Effects Hypothesis." *Social Forces* 79(2): 707–29.

Mears, Daniel P., and Avinash S. Bhati. 2006. "No Community Is an Island: The Effects of Resource Deprivation on Urban Violence in Spatially and Socially Proximate Communities." *Criminology* 44(3): 509–48.

Merton, Robert K. 1938. "Social Structure and Anomie." *American Sociological Review* 3(5): 672–82.

Messner, Steven F., Luc Anselin, Robert D. Baller, Darnell F. Hawkins, Glenn Deane, and Stewart E. Tolnay. 1999. "The Spatial Patterning of County Homicide Rates: An Application of Exploratory Spatial Data Analysis." *Journal of Quantitative Criminology* 15(4): 423–50.

Messner, Steven F., and Richard Rosenfeld. 2001. *Crime and the American Dream*, 3d ed. Belmont, Calif.: Wadsworth.

Messner, Steven F., and Kenneth Tardiff. 1986. "Economic Inequality and Levels of Homicide: An Analysis of Urban Neighborhoods." *Criminology* 24(2): 297–317.

Miller, Jody. 2008. *Getting Played: African American Girls, Urban Inequality, and Gendered Violence*. New York: New York University Press.

Morenoff, Jeffrey D., Robert J. Sampson, and Stephen W. Raudenbush. 2001. "Neighborhood Inequality, Collective Efficacy, and the Spatial Dynamics of Urban Violence." *Criminology* 39(3): 517–59.

Musto, David F. 1973. *The American Disease: Origins of Narcotic Control*. New Haven, Conn.: Yale University Press.

National Advisory Commission on Civil Disorders. 1968. *Report of the National Advisory Commission on Civil Disorders*. Washington: U.S. Government Printing Office.

National Center for Health Statistics. 2009. *Vital Statistics: Leading Causes of Death*, table LCWK4_2005. Available at: http://www.cdc.gov/nchs/data/dvs/LCWK4_2005.pdf (accessed February 24, 2010).

Nelsen, Candice, Jay Corzine, and Lin Huff-Corzine. 1994. "The Violent West Reexamined: A Research Note on Regional Homicide Rates." *Criminology* 32(1): 149–61.

Nielsen, Amy L., Matthew T. Lee, and Ramiro Martinez Jr. 2005. "Integrating Race, Place, and Motive in Social Disorganization Theory: Lessons from a Comparison of Black and Latino Homicide Types in Two Immigrant Destination Cities." *Criminology* 43(3): 837–72.

Oliver, Melvin L., and Thomas M. Shapiro. 2006. *Black Wealth/White Wealth: A New Perspective on Racial Inequality*, 10th anniv. ed. New York: Routledge.

Omi, Michael, and Howard Winant. 1994. *Racial Formation in the United States: From the 1960s to the 1990s*. New York: Routledge.

Orser, W. Edward. 1994. *Blockbusting in Baltimore: The Edmondson Village Story*. Lexington: University of Kentucky Press.

Osgood, D. Wayne. 2000. "Poisson-Based Regression Analysis of Aggregate Crime Rates." *Journal of Quantitative Criminology* 16(1): 21–43.

Pager, Devah. 2007. *Marked: Race, Crime, and Finding Work in an Era of Mass Incarceration*. Chicago: University of Chicago Press.

Pager, Devah, and Hana Shepherd. 2008. "The Sociology of Discrimination: Racial Discrimination in Employment, Housing, Credit, and Consumer Markets." *Annual Review of Sociology* 34(1): 181–209.

Parker, Karen F. 2004. "Polarized Labor Markets, Industrial Restructuring and Urban Violence: A Dynamic Model of the Economic Transformation and Urban Violence." *Criminology* 42(3): 619–45.

———. 2008. *Unequal Crime Decline: Theorizing Race, Urban Inequality, and Criminal Violence*. New York: New York University Press.

Parker, Karen F., and Matthew V. Pruitt. 2000. "How the West Was One: Explaining the Similarities in Race-Specific Homicide Rates in the West and South." *Social Forces* 78(4): 1483–1508.

Pastore, Ann L., and Kathleen Maguire, eds. 2009a. *Sourcebook of Criminal Justice Statistics*, tables 3.125.2005 and 3.127.2005. Available at: http://www.albany.edu/sourcebook/tost_3.html#3_aa (accessed March 11, 2009).

———, eds. 2009b. *Sourcebook of Criminal Justice Statistics*, tables 3.8.2006 and 3.9.2006. Available at: http://www.albany.edu/sourcebook/tost_3.html#3_aa (accessed March 11, 2009).

———, eds. 2009c. *Sourcebook of Criminal Justice Statistics*, tables 3.22.2006 and 3.23.2006. Available at: http://www.albany.edu/sourcebook/tost_3.html#3_aa (accessed March 11, 2009).

Pattillo, Mary. 2007. *Black on the Block: The Politics of Race and Class in the City.* Chicago: University of Chicago Press.

Pattillo-McCoy, Mary E. 1999. *Black Picket Fences: Privilege and Peril Among the Black Middle Class.* Chicago: University of Chicago Press.

Peterson, Ruth D. 1985. "Discriminatory Decision Making at the Legislative Level: An Analysis of the Comprehensive Drug Abuse Prevention and Control Act of 1970." *Law and Human Behavior* 9(3): 243–69.

Peterson, Ruth D., and Lauren J. Krivo. 2005. "Macro-Structural Analyses of Race, Ethnicity, and Violent Crime: Recent Lessons and New Directions for Research." *Annual Review of Sociology* 31(1): 331–56.

———. 2009a. "Race, Residence, and Violent Crime: A Structure of Inequality." *Kansas Law Review* 57(4): 903–33.

———. 2009b. "Segregated Spatial Locations, Race-Ethnic Composition, and Neighborhood Violent Crime." *Annals of the American Academy of Political and Social Science* 623(1): 93–107.

———. 2010. The National Neighborhood Crime Study, 2000 [computer file]. ICPSR27501-V1. Ann Arbor, Mich.: Inter-University Consortium for Political and Social Research [distributor]. 2010. doi:10.3886/ICPSR27501.

Peterson, Ruth D., Lauren J. Krivo, and Christopher R. Browning. 2006. "Segregation and Racial-Ethnic Inequality in Crime: New Directions." In *Taking Stock: The Status of Criminological Theory*, edited by Francis Cullen, John Wright, and Kristie Blevins. New Brunswick, N.J.: Transaction Press.

Peterson, Ruth D., Lauren J. Krivo, and Mark A. Harris. 2000. "Disadvantage and Neighborhood Violent Crime: Do Local Institutions Matter?" *Journal of Research in Crime and Delinquency* 37(1): 31–63.

Pfeifer, Michael J. 2004. *Rough Justice: Lynching and American Society, 1874–1947.* Chicago: University of Illinois Press.

Portes, Alejandro, and Rubén G. Rumbaut. 1996. *Immigrant America: A Portrait*, 2d ed. Berkeley: University of California Press.

powell, john a. 2007. "Structural Racism and Spatial Jim Crow." In *The Black Metropolis in the Twenty-first Century: Race, Power, and Politics of Place*, edited by Robert D. Bullard. Lanham, Md.: Rowman and Littlefield.

Pratt, Travis, and Francis Cullen. 2005. "Assessing Macro-Level Predictors and Theories of Crime: A Meta-Analysis." In *Crime and Justice: A Review of Research*, edited by Michael Tonry. Chicago: University of Chicago Press.

Price-Spratlen, Townsand, and Avery M. Guest. 2002. "Race and Population Change: A Longitudinal Look at Cleveland Neighborhoods, 1910–1990." *Sociological Forum* 17(1): 105–36.

Provine, Doris Marie. 2007. *Unequal Under Law: Race in the War on Drugs.* Chicago: University of Chicago Press.

Quillian, Lincoln. 2002. "Why Is Black-White Residential Segregation So Persistent? Evidence on Three Theories from Migration Data." *Social Science Research* 31(2): 197–229.

————. 2003. "The Decline of Male Employment in Low-Income Black Neighborhoods, 1950–1990." *Social Science Research* 32(2): 220–50.

Quillian, Lincoln, and Devah Pager. 2001. "Black Neighbors, Higher Crime? The Role of Racial Stereotypes in Evaluations of Neighborhood Crime." *American Journal of Sociology* 107(3): 717–67.

Reasons, Charles E., and William D. Perdue. 1981. *The Ideology of Social Problems.* Sherman Oaks, Calif.: Alfred Publishing.

Reskin, Barbara F. 2004. "The Discrimination System: Race and Public Policy." Paper presented to the annual meeting of the American Association of Law Schools. Atlanta (January 2).

Romero, Mary. 2006. "Racial Profiling and Immigration Law Enforcement: Rounding Up of Usual Suspects in the Latino Community." *Critical Sociology* 32(2–3): 449–75.

Roscigno, Vincent J. 1998. "Race and the Reproduction of Educational Disadvantage." *Social Forces* 76(3): 1033–60.

Rose, Dina R., and Todd R. Clear. 1998. "Incarceration, Social Capital, and Crime: Implications for Social Disorganization Theory." *Criminology* 36(3): 441–80.

Rosenbaum, Emily, and Samantha Friedman. 2001. "Differences in the Locational Attainment of Immigrant and Native-Born Households with Children in New York City." *Demography* 38(3): 337–48.

————. 2007. *The Housing Divide: How Generations of Immigrants Fare in New York's Housing Market.* New York: New York University Press.

Rosenfeld, Richard. 2002. "Crime Decline in Context." *Contexts* 1(1): 25–35.

Rosenfeld, Richard, Timothy M. Bray, and Arlen Egley. 1999. "Facilitating Violence: A Comparison of Gang-Motivated, Gang-Affiliated, and Nongang Youth Homicides." *Journal of Quantitative Criminology* 15(4): 495–516.

Rosenfeld, Richard, Robert Fornango, and Andres F. Rengifo. 2007. "The Impact of Order-Maintenance Policing on New York City Homicide and Robbery Rates: 1988–2001." *Criminology* 45(2): 355–83.

Ross, Stephen L., and Margery Austin Turner. 2005. "Housing Discrimination in Metropolitan America: Explaining Changes Between 1989 and 2000." *Social Problems* 52(2): 152–80.

Ross, Stephen, and John Yinger. 2002. *The Color of Credit: Mortgage Discrimination, Research Methodology, and Fair-Lending Enforcement.* Cambridge, Mass.: MIT Press.

Russell, Katheryn K. 1998. *The Color of Crime: Racial Hoaxes, White Fear, Black Protectionism, Police Harassment, and Other Macroaggressions.* New York: New York University Press.

Russell-Brown, Katheryn. 2004. *Underground Codes: Race, Crime, and Related Fires.* New York: New York University Press.

Sampson, Robert J. 1987. "Urban Black Violence: The Effect of Male Joblessness and Family Disruption." *American Journal of Sociology* 93(2): 348–82.

———. 2006. "Collective Efficacy Theory: Lessons Learned and Directions for Future Inquiry." In *Taking Stock: The Status of Criminological Theory*, edited by Francis Cullen, John Wright, and Kristie Blevins. New Brunswick, N.J.: Transaction Press.

———. 2008. "Rethinking Crime and Immigration." *Contexts* 7(1): 28–33.

———. 2009. "Racial Stratification and the Durable Tangle of Neighborhood Inequality." *Annals of the American Academy of Political and Social Science* 621(1): 260–80.

Sampson, Robert J., and Lydia Bean. 2006. "Cultural Mechanisms and Killing Fields: A Revised Theory of Community-Level Racial Inequality." In *The Many Colors of Crime: Inequalities of Race, Ethnicity, and Crime in America*, edited by Ruth D. Peterson, Lauren J. Krivo, and John Hagan. New York: New York University Press.

Sampson, Robert J., and W. Byron Groves. 1989. "Community Structure and Crime: Testing Social-Disorganization Theory." *American Journal of Sociology* 94(4): 774–802.

Sampson, Robert J., Jeffrey D. Morenoff, and Felton Earls. 1999. "Beyond Social Capital: Spatial Dynamics of Collective Efficacy for Children." *American Sociological Review* 64(5): 633–60.

Sampson, Robert J., and Stephen W. Raudenbush. 1999. "Systematic Social Observation of Public Spaces: A New Look at Disorder in Urban Neighborhoods." *American Journal of Sociology* 105(3): 603–51.

Sampson, Robert J., Stephen W. Raudenbush, and Felton Earls. 1997. "Neighborhoods and Violent Crime: A Multilevel Study of Collective Efficacy." *Science* 277(5328): 918–24.

Sampson, Robert J., Patrick Sharkey, and Stephen W. Raudenbush. 2008. "Durable Effects of Concentrated Disadvantage on Verbal Ability Among African-American Children." *Proceedings of the National Academy of Sciences* 105(3): 845–52.

Sampson, Robert J., and William Julius Wilson. 1995. "Toward a Theory of Race, Crime, and Urban Inequality." In *Crime and Inequality*, edited by John Hagan and Ruth D. Peterson. Stanford, Calif.: Stanford University Press.

Seligman, Amanda I. 2005. *Block by Block: Neighborhoods and Public Policy on Chicago's West Side.* Chicago: University of Chicago Press.

Shapiro, Thomas M. 2004. *The Hidden Cost of Being African American: How Wealth Perpetuates Inequality.* Oxford: Oxford University Press.

Shaw, Clifford, and Henry McKay. 1969. *Juvenile Delinquency and Urban Areas*, rev. ed. Chicago: University of Chicago Press.

Shihadeh, Edward S., and Wesley M. Shrum. 2004. "Serious Crime in Urban Neighborhoods: Is There a Race Effect?" *Sociological Spectrum* 24(4): 507–33.

Skogan, Wesley G. 1990. *Disorder and Decline: Crime and the Spiral of Decay in American Neighborhoods.* Berkeley: University of California Press.

Small, Mario Luis, and Monica McDermott. 2006. "The Presence of Organizational Resources in Poor Urban Neighborhoods: An Analysis of Average and Contextual Effects." *Social Forces* 84(3): 1697–1724.

Smelser, Neil J., William Julius Wilson, and Faith Mitchell. 2001. *America Becoming: Racial Trends and Their Consequences,* vols. 1 and 2. Washington, D.C.: National Academies Press.

Smith, Jessie, and Carrell Horton. 1997. *Statistical Record of Black America,* 4th ed. Detroit: Gale Research Press.

Smith, William R., Sharon Glave Frazee, and Elizabeth L. Davison. 2000. "Furthering the Integration of Routine Activity and Social Disorganization Theories: Small Units of Analysis and the Study of Street Robbery as a Diffusion Process." *Criminology* 38(2): 489–523.

Solis, Carmen, Edwardo L. Portillos, and Rod K. Brunson. 2009. "Latino Youths' Experiences with and Perceptions of Involuntary Police Encounters." *Annals of the American Academy of Political and Social Science* 623(1): 39–51.

Solorzano, Daniel G., and Armida Ornelas. 2002. "A Critical Race Analysis of Advanced Placement Classes: A Case of Educational Inequality." *Journal of Latinos and Education* 1(4): 215–26.

South, Scott J., Kyle Crowder, and Erick Chavez. 2005. "Exiting and Entering High-Poverty Neighborhoods: Latinos, Blacks, and Anglos Compared." *Social Forces* 84(2): 873–900.

South, Scott J., Kyle Crowder, and Jeremy Pais. 2008. "Inter-Neighborhood Migration and Spatial Assimilation in a Multi-Ethnic World: Comparing Latinos, Blacks, and Anglos." *Social Forces* 87(1): 415–43.

Spohn, Cassia. 2009. "Race, Sex, and Pretrial Detention in Federal Court: Indirect Effects and Cumulative Disadvantage." *University of Kansas Law Review* 57(4): 879–901.

Squires, Gregory D., and Charis E. Kubrin. 2006. *Privileged Places: Race, Residence, and the Structure of Opportunity.* Boulder, Colo.: Lynne Rienner Publishers.

Squires, Gregory D., and Sally O'Connor. 2001. *Color and Money: Politics and Prospects for the Community Reinvestment Movement in Urban America.* Albany: State University of New York Press.

St. John, Craig. 2002. "The Concentration of Affluence in the United States, 1990." *Urban Affairs Review* 37(4): 500–20.

Sullivan, Mercer. 1989. *Getting Paid: Youth Crime and Work in the Inner City.* Ithaca, N.Y.: Cornell University Press.

Sum, Andrew, Ishwar Khatiwada, Joseph McLaughlin, and Sheila Palma. 2009. "The Economic Recession of 2007–2009: A Comparative Perspective on Its Duration and the Severity of Its Labor Market Impacts." Working paper. Boston: Northeastern University, Center for Labor Market Studies. Available at: http://www.clms.neu.edu/publication/documents/Economic_Recession_of_20072009.pdf (accessed June 12, 2009).

Suttles, Gerald D. 1972. *The Social Construction of Communities.* Chicago: University of Chicago Press.

Taylor, Ralph B. 2001. *Breaking Away from Broken Windows: Baltimore Neighborhoods and the Nationwide Fight Against Crime, Grime, Fear, and Decline.* Boulder, Colo.: Westview Press.

Tita, George E., and Robert T. Greenbaum. 2009. "Crime, Neighborhoods, and Units of Analysis: Putting Space in Its Place." In *Putting Crime in Its Place: Units of Analysis in Geographic Criminology,* edited by David Weisburd, Wim Burnasco, and Gerben J. N. Bruinsma. New York: Springer.

Tolnay, Stewart E., and E. M. Beck. 1995. *A Festival of Violence: An Analysis of Southern Lynchings, 1882–1930.* Urbana: University of Illinois Press.

Tomaskovic-Devey, Donald. 1993. *Gender and Racial Inequality at Work: The Sources and Consequences of Job Segregation.* Ithaca, N.Y.: ILR Press.

Topalli, Volkan, Richard Wright, and Robert Fornango. 2002. "Drug Dealers, Robbery, and Retaliation." *British Journal of Criminology* 42(2): 337–51.

Twine, France Windance, and Jonathan W. Warren, eds. 2000. *Racing Research, Researching Race: Methodological Dilemmas in Critical Race Studies.* New York: New York University Press.

Tyler, Tom R., and Yuen J. Huo. 2002. *Trust in the Law: Encouraging Public Cooperation with the Police and Courts.* New York: Russell Sage Foundation.

U.S. Bureau of the Census. 1962. *Statistical Abstract of the United States: 1962,* table 299. Washington: U.S. Bureau of the Census. Available at: http://www2. census.gov/prod2/statcomp/documents/1962-04.pdf (accessed March 13, 2009).

———. 2007. *Census of Population and Housing, 2000: Summary File 3.* Available at: http://www.icpsr.umich.edu/CENSUS2000/summaryfile3.html (accessed March 3, 2010).

———. 2009a. *Population by Race and Hispanic or Latino Origin, for States, Puerto Rico, and Places of 100,000 or More Population: 2000,* table 4. Washington: U.S. Bureau of the Census. Available at: http://www.census.gov/population/ www/cen2000/briefs/phc-t6/index.html (accessed November 17, 2009).

———. 2009b. *Statistical Abstract of the United States: 2009,* table 596. Washington: U.S. Bureau of the Census. Available at: http://www.census.gov/compendia/ statab/cats/labor_force_employment_earnings.html (accessed March 13, 2009).

U.S. Commission on Civil Rights. 2005. *The Economic Stagnation of the Black Middle Class.* Washington: U.S. Commission on Civil Rights. Available at: http://www.usccr.gov/pubs/122805_BlackAmericaStagnation.pdf (accessed December 30, 2008).

U.S. Department of Justice. 2008a. *Crime in the United States, 2007,* table 43. Available at: http://www.fbi.gov/ucr/cius2007/data/table_43.html (accessed March 11, 2009).

———. 2008b. *Crime in the United States, 2007,* table 1. Available at: http:// www.fbi.gov/ucr/cius2007/data/table_01.html (accessed March 12, 2009).

Vélez, María. B. 2001. "The Role of Public Social Control in Urban Neighborhoods: A Multilevel Analysis of Victimization Risk." *Criminology* 39(4): 837–64.

———. 2006. "Toward an Understanding of the Lower Rates of Homicide in Latino Versus Black Neighborhoods: A Look at Chicago." In *The Many Colors of Crime: Inequalities of Race, Ethnicity, and Crime in America,* edited by Ruth D. Peterson, Lauren J. Krivo, and John Hagan. New York: New York University Press.

Venkatesh, Sudhir Alladi. 2006. *Off the Books: The Underground Economy of the Urban Poor.* Cambridge, Mass.: Harvard University Press.

Walker, Samuel, Cassia Spohn, and Miriam DeLone. 2007. *The Color of Justice: Race, Ethnicity, and Crime in America.* Belmont, Calif.: Thomson-Wadsworth.

Wallace, Deborah, and Roderick Wallace. 2001. *A Plague on Your Houses: How New York Was Burned Down and National Public Health Crumbled.* New York: Verso.

Weitzer, Ronald, and Steven A. Tuch. 2006. *Race and Policing in America: Conflict and Reform.* New York: Cambridge University Press.

Western, Bruce. 2006. *Punishment and Inequality in America.* New York: Russell Sage Foundation.

Wilkes, Rima, and John Iceland. 2004. "Hypersegregation in the Twenty-first Century." *Demography* 41(1): 23–36.

Wilkinson, Deanna L. 2003. *Guns, Violence, and Identity Among African American and Latino Youth.* New York: LFB Scholarly Publishing.

Wilkinson, Deanna L., Chauncey C. Beaty, and Regina M. Lurry. 2009. "Youth Violence—Crime or Self-Help? Marginalized Urban Males' Perspectives on the Limited Efficacy of the Criminal Justice System to Stop Youth Violence." *Annals of the American Academy of Political and Social Science* 623(1): 25–38.

Williams, Richard, Reynold Nesiba, and Eileen Diaz McConnell. 2005. "The Changing Face of Inequality in Home Mortgage Lending." *Social Problems* 52(2): 181–208.

Wilson, William Julius. 1987. *The Truly Disadvantaged: The Inner City, the Underclass, and Public Policy.* Chicago: University of Chicago Press.

———. 1996. *When Work Disappears: The World of the New Urban Poor.* New York: Knopf.

———. 2009. *More Than Just Race: Being Black and Poor in the Inner City.* New York: Norton.

Wolfgang, Marvin M., and Franco Ferracuti. 1967. *The Subculture of Violence.* London: Tavistock.

Wooldredge, John, and Amy Thistlethwaite. 2003. "Neighborhood Structure and Race-Specific Rates of Intimate Assault." *Criminology* 41(2): 393–422.

Wyly, Elvin K., and Steven R. Holloway. 1999. "The *Color of Money* Revisited: Racial Lending Patterns in Atlanta's Neighborhoods." *Housing Policy Debate* 10(3): 555–600.

Yinger, John. 1995. *Closed Doors, Opportunities Lost: The Continuing Costs of Housing Discrimination.* New York: Russell Sage Foundation.

Young, Robert L. 1991. "Race, Conceptions of Crime and Justice, and Support for the Death Penalty." *Social Psychology Quarterly* 54(1): 67–75.

Young, Vernetta. 2006. "Demythologizing the 'Criminalblackman': The Carnival Mirror." In *The Many Colors of Crime: Inequalities of Race, Ethnicity, and Crime in America,* edited by Ruth D. Peterson, Lauren J. Krivo, and John Hagan. New York: New York University Press.

Zatz, Marjorie S., and Hilary Smith. 2008. "Immigration, Crime, and Justice: Rhetoric, Reality, and Ramifications of Recent U.S. Immigration Policies." Paper presented to the conference "The Paradoxes of Race, Law, and Inequality in the United States." University of California, Irvine (May 2–3).

Zavodny, Madeline. 1999. "Determinants of Recent Immigrants' Locational Choices." *International Migration Review* 33(4): 1014–30.

Zuberi, Tukufu. 2001. *Thicker Than Blood: How Racial Statistics Lie.* Minneapolis: University of Minnesota Press.

Zuberi, Tukufu, and Eduardo Bonilla-Silva. 2008a. "Telling the Real Tale of the Hunt: Toward a Race-Conscious Sociology of Racial Stratification." In *White Logic, White Methods: Racism and Methodology,* edited by Tukufu Zuberi and Eduardo Bonilla-Silva. New York: Rowman and Littlefield.

———, eds. 2008b. *White Logic, White Methods: Racism and Methodology,* edited by Tukufu Zuberi and Eduardo Bonilla-Silva. New York: Rowman and Littlefield.

$=$ Index $=$